Digital Minimalism in Everyday Life

Learn to Break Your Tech Habits, Clear Your Head, and Take Back Your Life
(2022 Guide for Beginners)

Gale Feron

i

Contents

INTRODUCTION

Minimalism is fundamentally about doing more with less. It is a philosophical decision rather than merely an aesthetic one.

The goal of digital minimalism is to reduce your reliance on the internet, smartphones, computers, and other devices to regain control over your intentions, focus, and freedom to choose.

This book was inspired by lessons and ideas presented by Cal Newport in his book ***Digital Minimalism: Choosing a Focused Life in a Noisy World.***

I hope you don't mind if I agree with him that digital minimalism is a philosophy centered on the use of technology. I also believe that we should all practice digital decluttering, deprive ourselves of solitude on occasion, limit our social media exposure (if not eliminate it), and prioritize real-world experience over synthetic associations in the digital world.

In this book, I only briefly discuss the impact of digital media on adults and children. I even present some numbers to back up the points I've made. However, because Cal Newport has already done such an excellent job on the subject, I do not dwell on it extensively in this book. To put it another way, there is no need to reinvent the wheel.

What I'd rather present in this work are actionable steps, tips, and tricks that you can take on your own to deal with the challenges of technology addiction on your terms in your daily life.

This is a book for ordinary people who don't always understand psychological and other technical jargon. A great deal of effort has gone into making this book as jargon-free as possible.

However, where jargon is used in these pages, it is accompanied by explanations that are understandable to the average person.

This book is about living a digital minimalist lifestyle. I've also borrowed some ideas from Newport to explain how digital media and technology affect us as humans. On the other hand, I depart from his theoretical foundation and focus on how to apply digital minimalism in everyday situations.

Section two of this book, for example, begins with a digital inventory and decluttering. It is then followed by methods for performing a digital detox. You will also learn mindfulness techniques to help you stay focused and in the present moment.

Other techniques and strategies will be covered, such as taking a tech sabbatical, doing art therapy, creative work, and digital communication.

Remember that developing new habits and breaking old ones takes time. As a result, the strategies and techniques you'll learn here aren't one-time fixes. You must devote time to trying and practicing them so that they become a part of the new you.

Section One

Concept Definition and Understanding

Chapter One

What Exactly Is Digital Minimalism?

Minimalism is a term that is frequently used these days. Digital minimalism is one interpretation of this philosophy or way of life.

But, before we get into its "digital" aspects, let's first define minimalism.

Understanding the fundamental concepts of a minimalist lifestyle will help you comprehend digital minimalism.

What Exactly Is Minimalism?

You've probably heard people describe a minimalist lifestyle.

Some believe it means you can only own a hundred items and nothing more. Others argue that practicing minimalism requires you to give up your job.

As you read through the various descriptions, you might get the impression that it's some kind of mystical or exotic way of life. The photos of minimalist homes are very appealing.

However, starting a blog, not having children, and not owning a phone seems far-fetched for ordinary people like you and me. But there is one point I'd like to emphasize:

That is not the case with a minimalist lifestyle.

To be honest, that is not what minimalism is all about. Some may dismiss minimalism as a fad in home organization. Some may even believe it is an overly restrictive way of life.

Some people claim that they are unable to adopt a minimalist lifestyle due to the aforementioned rules and restrictions. Just keep in mind that being a minimalist has nothing to do with any of those things.

Yes, practicing minimalism can help you live with less clutter in your life. That, however, is not the point.

Consider minimalism to be a tool.

What is it used for if it is a tool? You use it to achieve liberation. It is your doorway to freedom from worrying, fear, feeling overwhelmed, consumer culture, and even depression.

Keep in mind, however, that minimalism does not condemn material possessions. There's nothing wrong with wanting to own a car (or two), a house, a cell phone, or a shoe collection.

You don't want your possessions to become the center of your universe. We sometimes place far too much value on what we own and have, neglecting other equally important factors such as your health, mental and emotional well-being, relationships, and personal growth.

Do you want a rewarding and successful career? Then go ahead and work toward your career objectives. Do you want to raise children and have a happy family? Do you want a brand-new car and a million-dollar mansion?

Minimalism encourages such things. However, this philosophy or way of life helps you decide to own or work on those things deliberately and consciously.

Here is a very simplified definition of a minimalist lifestyle that anyone should be able to understand:

"It is a lifestyle choice in which one eliminates life's excesses to focus on aspects of living that are equally important and contribute to freedom, fulfillment, and true happiness."

Personal Experiences with Minimalism

From personal experience, a minimalist lifestyle is difficult to begin and difficult to maintain. But it depends on the individual—I have friends who have successfully transitioned to a minimalist lifestyle.

It has aided me in the following ways:

- Discover my life's purpose

- Remove all unnecessary items from my life.

- Contribute to causes and things that are bigger and more important than me.

- Reduce my focus and assist me in learning to help others.

- Find happiness in your life.

- Personal development

- Concentrate on my mental and physical health.

- Activate my creative side

- Consume less and contribute to environmental preservation.

- Feel genuine freedom (no longer living the nine-to-five life)

- Explore various interests.

- Be present at the moment and enjoy what I have. Do not let greed overcome my desires.

- Reclaim time for me and Eliminate discontent no matter what situation I'm in You could say that since successfully implementing a minimalist lifestyle, I've discovered true and lasting happiness.

And I hope you will accomplish the same.

I've discovered that my possessions do not provide me with long-term happiness. Life itself has brought me happiness. The good news is that determining your level of happiness is entirely up to you.

Minimalism in the Digital Age

Digital minimalism is defined as minimalist living in the digital age. It has grown in popularity as our modern lives have become increasingly centered on technology. The rise of smartphones, tablets, and other personalized technology has had an impact on us in much the same way that our possessions and other material things did previously. You might think that minimalists like me are exaggerating, but if you look at our personalized technology (cellphones, for example), you'll notice that we have an unhealthy relationship with it.

Someone once said that in a world where we have made global interconnectivity possible, humans have become more distant from one another. Artificial digital connections have replaced human connections, and our reliance on these things has become quite addictive.

Advantages of Minimalism in General

Before we go any further, I'd like to highlight some of the general benefits of minimalist living. Following that, we will discuss what digital minimalism is specifically, what its core principles are, and what it would be like if you tried it right now.

Remember that minimalism is a lifestyle choice that prompts you to consider what specific items truly add value to your life. This is the fundamental rule you will follow when practicing digital minimalism. Here are some of the advantages of living a minimalist lifestyle in general:

1. You save more money because you spend less money.

When you practice minimalism in your life, you make a conscious decision to spend your money only on things that you require. That doesn't mean you won't treat yourself to some luxuries. You will spend money on fun and games as well, but you will be more conscious of your spending habits. You'll learn to avoid unplanned vacation splurges, impulsive shopping, and other financial excesses.

You will end up saving money because you will spend less on things you don't need.

2. Decrease stress

Living with less means not having to worry about as many things.

You are not required to keep up with the Kardashians or whoever it is that people are expected to keep up with. In terms of digital minimalism, you don't have to worry about how many likes your post receives, how many views your videos receive, who is watching your news feed, etc.

The bottom line is that you learn to be yourself no matter who looks at your profile or what others think or say about you online.

3. You feel more clear and clean.

When was the last time you looked at how many icons you had on your computer? Have you noticed how much junk is on your hard drive? What images and movies do you have saved in your folders?

The first time I attempted to declutter, the result was profound. I saw my house for the first time in my life with wide open spaces. My computer desktop screen looked nice, and I could see the wallpaper image I chose.

The same was true for my phone. Everything had become more organized. It gave me the impression that I was off to a new beginning—and it was. It was a uniquely clean slate feeling that made me realize I was on my way to better times.

4. A stronger sense of freedom

The liberating feeling that comes from having clear and clean spaces at home and work. It gives you a greater sense of independence. Furthermore, it influences your productivity—there is no longer any clutter to contend with, so you end up becoming more productive at home and work.

5. You have the opportunity to help others by supporting a cause.

When I first started decluttering, one of the first things I did was visit a local homeless shelter. I had so much stuff, including clothes, food in storage (food I didn't want to eat), tools and equipment, and even old gadgets I hadn't used in years.

My old computer screen, as well as several keyboards and other computer accessories, were donated to charity. They were using it in one of their offices as of the last time I checked.

I gathered them all and gave them to the shelter. Helping others made me feel better about myself.

Furthermore, because I no longer throw out a lot of garbage, I believe I am doing my part to help preserve the environment.

6. Prioritize quality over quantity.

I've noticed that people who practice any form of minimalism tend to prioritize the quality of their possessions, including clothing, food, and even the apps they download.

You are no longer compelled to purchase the most recent phone model or gadget. You learn to put the principle of delayed gratification into practice. You wait until you are certain that the phone you are interested in is true of high quality.

If it falls short of your expectations, keep your old phone (or whatever gadget it is). If your equipment is still functioning properly, there is no reason to replace it with a brand new item.

You are more conscious of your choices, and as a result, you place a higher value on the quality of the products you buy, whether they are software or other types of technology.

7. More rest time

You have more time to take care of yourself and rest because you don't waste time on things.

8. Make more meaningful investments.

You can devote more time and effort to making your home look exactly how you want it to. You're not bound by the past, and you're not concerned about the future, so you can concentrate on more important things.

Important Details in Digital Minimalism

We can now delve deeper into the details after discussing what minimalism is, the benefits it can provide, and how it applies to our digital lives. Just keep in mind that digital minimalism is the application of minimalist philosophy and lifestyle to our use of technology.

Cal Newport, a computer science professor at Georgetown University, is a leading figure in the world of digital minimalism. He defines digital minimalism as "a philosophy that helps you question what digital communication tools (and behaviors associated with these tools) add the most value to your life."

According to Newport's definition, digital minimalism does not only apply or refer to the digital technology that we use, but it also refers to our attitudes toward the digital technologies that we have at our disposal.

Our digital tools and products, like physical, emotional, or psychological issues, can become an impediment to us. They cause us to lose focus, worry excessively, and sometimes overthink things. They can even stress us out or, on the other hand, make us rely on and become addicted to technology.

In this regard, we can say that adopting digital minimalism as a lifestyle can be a healthy response, particularly when dealing with potentially addictive or dependent behavior. We assess not only the type of technology that we use, but also our behaviors, emotions, and attitudes toward digital technology. Practicing it entails paying attention to the tradeoffs we make, the signs and signals of tech addiction, and our reliance on it.

Essential Digital Minimalism Principles

When it comes to our digital lives, minimalism adheres to a few fundamental principles. Consider the primary goals driving the practices and tips you'll find in the later chapters of this book.

People are always prioritized over technology.

We live in a time when the internet and social media are supposed to bring people closer together. We live in an increasingly interconnected world. However, despite the digital connections that have been made available to us, we as humans are becoming increasingly disconnected.

These technologies, on the other hand, have become a force of isolation. A common scene depicted is an entire family sitting together in a living room, but each family member has his face buried in a screen.

Where is the human element in that? We may be digitally connected, but we appear to be emotionally, socially, and mindfully disconnected. We are, as they say, distracted by our screens. Our attention is so focused on the device in our hands and front of our eyes that we fail to recognize the true nature of our relationship with the people in front of us.

So, the first rule of digital minimalism is that people always come first. If we need to interact with someone in the same room, we should do it the old-fashioned way: we should talk.

Some people are realizing that while digital communication is great, nothing can replace face-to-face interaction. There is something about face-to-face interaction that we all crave, and people are starting to realize how lacking digital communication truly is.

For example, Antony Cauvin was featured in a BBC news report for inventing a "cuddle curtain" that allowed him to hug his grandmother. The video, which was shared on Facebook, moved many people.

In a similar story, Paige, a ten-year-old girl, had a brilliant idea: she made her own "hug curtain" The curtain she made was not medical or a product recommended by the CDC. Ziploc bags, a shower curtain, plastic plates, and a glue gun were all used to make it. Her hug curtain was hung in their front doorway, allowing her to physically hug her family and cuddle with grandma and grandpa.

People crave that one-on-one interaction. It's just human nature. And science may have a plausible explanation.

It's a condition known as touch deprivation. What happens when we are supported, loved, and emotionally touched? It doesn't have to be a hug, but that can also be beneficial. Sometimes all we need is a friendly pat on the back, a supportive rub on the shoulder, someone to hold our hand, or at the very least someone to lean on.

Dr. Katalin Gothard, a neuroscientist, believes that touch starvation is a type of withdrawal that anyone can experience. Direct person-to-person contact causes the brain to release oxytocin and opioids. Without human touch, no matter how insignificant, the brain produces fewer endogenous opioids and oxytocin.

This is one of the reasons we adopt dogs and other animals. We all want to have that one-on-one interaction with another creature. This personal contact reduces our heart rate and strengthens our immune system.

Dr. Colter Ray of San Diego State University explains that when we are deprived of something as basic as direct human interaction and the accompanying friendly touch, our bodies communicate to us what we are missing. Sometimes we simply look beyond the mark and miss the message entirely. We become dissatisfied, and at times even depressed.

This is because the brain no longer produces essential hormones such as serotonin.

This first fundamental rule of digital minimalism perfectly fits in to address this fundamental human need—that genuine person-to-person connection. That is why we must learn to prioritize people over technology.

Intentional Application of Technology

Our use of digital technology has sometimes become habitual. So, when you wake up in the morning, what is the first thing you do? Is it as simple as reaching for your phone to silence the alarm? Perhaps you're old-fashioned and still reach for an alarm clock to turn it off.

What is the first thing you do when you arrive at work? Do you go through your emails? When you get home from work, what is the first thing you do? Do you like to sit on the couch and watch television? What is Netflix's most recent hit show?

Our use of digital technology has indeed become habitual today. We may not realize it at times, but one of the first things we do is reach for our phones and check social media.

Here's a fact: digital technology has evolved into a major force in our lives. It is becoming more powerful as well as more widely available. It is relatively inexpensive (depending on the type of phone you use). On top of that, it is highly addictive.

Experts now use a variety of terms to describe this type of experience. It is also referred to as internet addiction, smartphone addiction, and other terms. To keep things simple, we'll refer to these phenomena collectively as "technology addiction."

In subsequent chapters of this book, we will discuss each of these conditions and provide you with signs and symptoms to help you determine if you have them. We will also provide practical and actionable tips to help you reduce symptoms and break free from your reliance on technology.

For the time being, just remember that one of the fundamental concepts or principles of digital minimalism is that your use of technology—any form of technology—should be mindful. It must be a deliberate decision, not the result of a long-held habit.

It is easier to break free from the bad or overuse of digital technology when we are intentional about our technology use. We can better determine what we truly value in life and make better decisions based on that determination. Our use of technology will eventually be purposeful and intentional.

Digital technology is a tool for creativity.

Our addiction to digital technology is based on the stimuli it provides. Some people have become so reliant on their gadgets that they only use them to make themselves feel better. This brief self-evaluation can be completed quickly. It won't take long.

Try to answer the following questions for yourself:

1. Do you get bored when you don't use your phone?

2. Do you feel compelled to play phone games when the world around you is uninteresting?

3. Do you frequently find yourself checking your social media even when you're talking to someone right in front of you?

4. Do you believe that if you don't use your phone, your day is incomplete?

If you answered yes to any of these questions, you may have developed a dependency on digital technology. It's not just your smartphone, computer, iPad, or tablet. It can be the same reassuring feeling when watching Netflix, your web TV, or another device, such as any Alexa-powered device, such as the Amazon Echo or Echo Dot.

Here's a common response that some people are probably used to hearing.

You are angry, sad, anxious, tired, upset, or experiencing any other type of discomfort. The first thing you do is seek relief—where do you find it?

You can play a game on your phone, watch a YouTube video, chat with your friends, make a short video on TikTok, take an Instagram selfie, or simply check your email again, even if you've already done so a hundred times.

But first and foremost, why do we do it? We use it to avoid discomfort, sadness, boredom, and other unpleasant emotions. In a nutshell, it is a quick fix. However, a quick fix is insufficient.

Experts believe that if we continue to do so, we will only cause ourselves to suffer in the long run. A quick fix is nothing more than a temporary gate that allows us to escape. The more we do it, the more difficult it becomes to confront the actual problem.

The good news is that there is a choice.

So, what are your options? The other option is to recognize that digital technology is a creative tool that should be used as such. We must stop using this technology to provide cheap relief from pain and discomfort. We should start using technology to make things that are meaningful, valuable, useful, and important.

When a minimalist lifestyle and philosophy are applied to one's digital life, you gain the same benefits as described previously for minimalism in general. You will gain freedom, more free space on your devices, more time for yourself, fewer worries, less stress, and more opportunities for the things that are important to you.

Important Takeaways

Minimalism is a way of life and a philosophy that believes that having less is more.

One of the emotional and psychological benefits of digital minimalism is regaining control over your power to choose and decreasing your reliance on digital technology.

Digital minimalism does not imply that you will stop using your phone; rather, you will use your digital devices with purpose and intention rather than impulsively.

Chapter 2

The Addiction to Technology

Important Note: In this chapter, we will discuss a variety of behavioral addictions, including technology, smartphones, social media, internet addiction, and others. Please keep in mind that there is a push to classify these behaviors as an established illnesses.

However, according to the DSM-IV (1995) or DSM-V, they are not yet officially recognized as a disorder or illness (2013). It is important to note that the Diagnostic and Statistical Manual of Mental Disorders (DSM) is the authoritative guide used by psychiatrists and other mental health professionals.

Because of the addictive nature of the behavior, we refer to them as addictions in this book, even though they are not yet officially recognized as such. We might have to wait a while before medical professionals officially recognize these behaviors as disorders.

Let us now proceed with the discussion.

It may take some effort to finally admit that we are addicted to digital technology. It manifests itself in a variety of ways, including smartphone, social media, internet, and videogame addiction.

These technologies share some characteristics. They were designed to be used daily and capture people's attention.

Because of a variety of rewards programmed into the entire system, you become more addicted to them as they steal your awareness and attention.

What exactly is technology addiction?

Addiction to technology is a type of behavioral addiction. It may sound like a harsh description, but mental health professionals classify it alongside other addictive behaviors such as sex and gambling.

According to experts, it is similar to substance abuse.

The main difference, of course, is that the individual is not dependent on any substance (e.g., drugs, alcohol, tobacco, etc.).

It is distinguished by an inability to limit, regulate, or control one's use of digital technology. This lack of control is also progressive, which means that as you continue to engage in this addictive behavior, you may lose even more control.

Some experts believe that technology addiction shares characteristics with other behaviors such as obsessive-compulsive disorder.

Profit = attracting attention

In many ways, you could say that grabbing attention is the lifeblood of digital technology. If their products are ineffective at maintaining your focus and attention, the companies that make them will lose money. This formula is used by tech titans such as Netflix, Amazon, Facebook, and Google to achieve long-term growth, increased revenues, and a high level of success.

The evolution of digital technology and how it is used for profit has raised numerous ethical concerns. Are these companies using technology to manipulate their customers? Isn't it true that people should have more power? Isn't the general public supposed to be made aware of how addictive technology can be?

Humans have been vulnerable to various forms of behavioral addiction since time immemorial. However, what digital technology has done in our time is amplify the aforementioned human tendencies.

In many cases, our addiction to various things has caused people to miss out on important life events. The majority of these moments are ones that you will never be able to relive or experience again.

Technology Addiction Types

There are various kinds of technology addictions. Among them are the following:

- Online auction addiction

- Addiction to gambling games (e.g., online gambling)

- Addiction to video consumption (e.g., YouTube, Netflix, Hulu, etc.)

- Shopping addiction (e.g., purchasing items on eBay and Amazon)

- Addiction to social media

- Addiction to video games

Many of these digital or technology addictions have an impact on certain critical parts of our brain, specifically the pleasure center. Some of these technological addictions cause severe physical symptoms, while others cause emotional and psychological distress.

However, our reliance on these various digital technologies does not cause us any direct harm. However, as our reliance on them grows, their impact on us can be quite overwhelming.

Why Is Digital Technology So Compulsive?

Why is digital technology so dominating? It's extremely addictive.

Digital addiction, like any other type of addiction, appeals to the pleasure center of the human brain. Because it is a behavioral addiction, it produces a short-term reward [7] and entices us to repeat the same behavior.

When you use (or overuse) technology, you get the equivalent of dopamine and/or serotonin release, which behavioral experts say is the same high or pleasure that you get from gambling, drugs, and other things that can lead to addiction.

It is important to note that several important factors interact to feed technology addiction and behavioral addiction in general.

Key Factors Contributing to Digital Addiction

The following are the key elements that contribute to the addictive nature of digital technology. And, more often than not, each of these elements feeds off the others.

They are as follows:

- Distraction

- Boredom is a huge need that can be met in a variety of ways. Marketers use the term "exploit" to describe something that is not necessarily bad. That is, to capitalize on a need to generate profits. For example, when a band releases a new album, the producers look for ways to "exploit" the new product (i.e., find ways to profit from it).

They would then use the material for traditional and digital radio airplay, album sales, individual song sales, use of the music in commercials and movies, and royalties on the lyrics or the music (which are two different things).

Boredom is similar in that you fill a need or void when you have nothing to do. People would go to any length to avoid that sensation.

People will do things that will entertain them, and, surprisingly, people will continue to do unpleasant things.

The use of social media and smartphones is a prime example of this phenomenon. Some people use it to distract themselves. Everyone does not feel great after using social media. Many Facebook users report feeling less happy after using the platform, but they continue to use it.

Why do people continue to use Facebook (or any other social media platform) despite the negative consequences?

Again, people will do anything to be distracted, no matter what the cost. According to experts, we do it because we would do anything to avoid boredom.

Variable Compensation

Why are gambling and chance games so addictive? Why do people continue to play slot machines even though there is no winning strategy? The reason for this is that these games offer variable rewards, which heightens the anticipation of the reward.

The same is true for social media. You never know how many people will react to a photo, video, message, comment, event, or anything else you post. The reward is finally delivered once you see how many likes, reactions, shares, and other vanity metrics you receive from that post.

The number of social media notifications you receive varies as well. It piques your interest because the outcome is unique each time.

You start to wonder, "OK, so how many people will like this one?" Is this one of my coolest photos? I'm curious how many people will react to this.

There are times when you have none, times when you have ten, and times when you have a hundred. One photo may receive three likes, but the next time you post, you may receive 300 or more, which will fuel your anticipation and excitement. When someone likes your latest video or photo update, don't you feel satisfied?

The reward is the feedback you get from social media, which makes the behavior very appealing, which is why we keep doing it.

The reward is variable, and it is similar to gambling. It is very appealing, and you risk very little financially, but you invest a lot in terms of psychology and attention. In short, once you get started, it is extremely difficult to beat.

Metrics of Vanity

We mentioned vanity metrics in the previous section. This refers to the number of likes, dislikes, and other responses we receive on social media. In a nutshell, digital technology feeds your vanity. Five hundred people like your day's outfit (OOTD). Two hundred people shared your post in which you criticized the government's handling of a specific situation.

You now have a thousand followers, which is a significant achievement.

Isn't this a huge victory?

These ostensible victories feed your conceit. It's fine to feed our ego; we all need it from time to time. However, when it becomes persistent and out of control, it can lead to social media or technology addiction.

On top of that, metrics (numerical and tangible measurement) validate your vanity. Getting a lot of reactions on social media is similar to getting a lot of dopamine hits.

When you are satisfied with an experience, you tend to repeat it to re-experience the reward. In other words, you seek that dopamine high over and over again. This is known as dopamine-driven feedback.

However, it is not limited to social media. Other digital technologies have the same effect. You can get the same pleasure hits when using other forms of digital media and digital technology, such as unlocking your smartphone].

When it comes to other types of digital media and content, there are also vanity metrics of some kind. We check our email inboxes, play games, ask Alexa questions, and shop (or window shop) online out of habit to receive the same pleasurable reward, no matter how large or small.

Content That Never Ends

Netflix introduced its auto-play feature in 2012. So to speak, it was a binge-watching revolution. It was the first time that any video-on-demand or video-streaming service offered nonstop entertainment. Needless to say, it was a huge success, and it made a lot of money.

Other digital media content providers quickly followed suit.

Facebook and YouTube both implemented the same feature. You can now scroll through hundreds upon hundreds of pieces of content indefinitely.

This is one of the main reasons why you end up spending 30 minutes to an hour on social media when all you wanted to do was watch that funny cat video your best friend posted two minutes ago. The strange thing about it all is that you become so engrossed in it that you forget what you were doing in the first place.

The Roots of Digital Addiction

Different factors contribute to digital or technology addiction.

Sometimes the causes differ from person to person.

It can take a variety of factors for a person to become dependent on certain technologies.

The following are some of the most common causes of technology addiction:

1. Depression: Depression can sometimes trigger a person's dependence and eventual addiction to technology. The strange thing is that our experience with technology feeds our depression, creating a vicious cycle. Some people get satisfaction from using the internet and temporarily forget about their problems. Their experience on social media can sometimes feed their depression, but they continue to use it as a form of release for them.

2. The Gang and Friend Effect: Some children use gaming and social media to make friends, which is sometimes acceptable. However, when children use digital technology excessively and in place of actual interactions with real-life friends, it becomes a habit. Some children spend countless hours online playing role-playing games to strengthen their game characters to attract more online friends whom they have never met in real life.

3. Social Anxiety and Shyness: Some people behave differently online. When they interact with other people online, it's as if they've developed a new personality. Some people who are naturally shy or who suffer from social anxiety may turn to the internet to escape their fears. Some of the shyest people can express themselves better online as if their online avatars serve as a shield or cover.

4. Expression of Other Addictions: Addictions can sometimes feed into one another. For example, if a person was a shopaholic in the past, they may transition to internet shopping and then to social media addiction as another manifestation of their previous dependencies.

Digital Technology's Impact and How It Affects Us

Surprisingly, many people are unaware of how much time they spend on their digital devices. If you look at the statistics, you might be surprised at how devastating this technology is.

According to researchers, people check their smartphones
or mobile devices every six minutes on average. You can't
wait any longer to see what's going on on the internet. We
adults also check our phones 150 times per day on average .

Influence on Cognitive Ability

Smartphone use also reduces human cognitive capacity.
Finally, digital technology addiction affects us in the same
way that drugs do, impairing our ability to think for
ourselves.

Experts believe that another underlying reason for the
addictive nature of digital media and technology is that they
feed human impulses while limiting our intentions.

The Effect on Children

Take note that this is the effect on adults. When our
children are involved, the situation becomes much worse.
According to one report, Apple's marketing was so effective
that 40% of US children under the age of nine have their
iPad.

Children of the same age group also spend more time on mobile devices. From 2011 to 2017, there is an 860% increase in time spent. They spend more time on small screens than they do with their peers. This decreases their social skills and playing violent video games reduces their ability to empathize with others. If you think you're overusing your phone, reconsider. According to experts, all children under the age of 18 use their smartphones nearly twice as much as adults. This reliance, if you will, on smartphones and other digital devices has now influenced how people deal with their relationships. As a result, it has made a lot of people unhappy. Instead of strengthening bonds, it has increased loneliness, particularly among the younger generation.

Changes in Brain Structure and Chemical Alterations

Internet addiction has been shown to cause structural changes in the brain as well as chemical changes. A person's ability to connect with attention, cognitive control, emotional processing, and decision-making is affected by structural changes.

According to research, parts of the brain that deal with a person's ability to pay attention (e.g., dorsolateral prefrontal cortex and orbitofrontal cortex) have lower levels of grey matter in people who are addicted to the internet.

According to studies, internet addiction impairs the proper connection and processing between different hemispheres of the brain.

Dopamine transporter levels in the brain have also been found to decrease in a technology-addicted brain. What does this imply? The more addicted you become to technology, the less satisfaction you get from it. That is, you tend to seek more and different forms of that behavior to experience the pleasure (or dopamine rush) that you are anticipating.

Consuming the same type of internet porn, for example, will become less appealing over time. To get the desired satisfaction from that type of digital media, the internet porn addict will look for other types of porn.

Similarly, the same games will not be as appealing as before.

The same social media posts will not be as humorous or entertaining.

You'll seek out more variants just to relive the good feelings you used to have.

I would like to invite you to read Cal Newport's book Digital Minimalism: *Choosing a Focused Life in a Noisy World* to learn more about the impact and influence of digital technology on our children and us. It is a comprehensive work that reveals how complicated our relationship with modern technology is.

As previously stated, this book focuses on actionable solutions and tips that you can implement right now at home to reduce and eventually eliminate your reliance on digital technology.

In the following section of this book, we will go over specific strategies that you can use at home and work.

The Effects of Technology Addiction on Human Life

The following are some of the negative effects of technology addiction on human life:

- Obesity

- Excessive weight loss

- Neck ache

- Personal hygiene issues

- Unhealthy eating habits

- Insomnia

- The carpal tunnel syndrome

- Headaches

- Backache

- Boredom when doing something other than watching digital media

- Fcar and loneliness

- Swings in mood

- Responsibility disruption and deferment

- Ignoring work

- A lot of time was wasted.

- Isolation from social networks

- When using the internet, I experience euphoria.

- Anxiety

- Guilt /Depression

Important Takeaways

All of us, especially our children, are affected by digital addiction.

It is addictive because it stimulates the brain's pleasure centers.

Digital addiction has a wide-ranging impact on us, feeding our anxieties, depression, and other conditions.

Section two

Digital Minimalism in Daily Life

Chapter 3

How to Conduct a Digital Inventory and De-Clutter

One of the most important things you should do as you practice digital minimalism is to take inventory and declutter. Keep in mind that digital minimalism is an ongoing process. It is not a one-time occurrence. It's something you'll have to work on all the time.

Our digital life, like physical clutter, is prone to entropy.

When you leave things alone—your bookcase, your kitchen, and even your bedroom—things tend to pile up without your knowledge.

You occasionally forget to put a cup away before leaving for work.

Maybe you forgot to put the laundry from yesterday in the hamper, or maybe you forgot to organize the groceries the other day.

You may even forget to prepare your bed before going to bed and after waking up in the morning.

Don't be concerned. Allow yourself to forgive yourself for these blunders.

They are natural and occur from time to time.

That is the purpose of minimalist living. Because you own fewer items, there won't be as much clutter as there was previously.

Things pile up from time to time in the case of digital minimalism.

This could include apps that were once necessary for work but are no longer required by your boss. It's also possible that you downloaded files in places where they're easy to find, such as your home or desktop screen.

Everything is forgiven.

It Isn't Just you don't worry; you'll get through it. It appears that this is a widespread phenomenon. Here are some statistics that may help you:

Since 2013, total global digital media usage has increased by 40%.

Every day, the average person will spend at least (at least!) three hours staring at his or her phone (or another mobile device).

People will spend one minute on social media for every five minutes they spend each day, regardless of the platform.

One minute of every two minutes spent nowadays will be spent on online entertainment. This includes watching videos on YouTube or other video streaming services, as well as listening to music, playing games, and engaging in other forms of online entertainment.

In the last three years, total smartphone usage has more than doubled.

These trends will continue unless we take action.

Managing Digital Entropy

And because everything is subject to entropy—that phenomenon in which everything simply returns to utter chaos—you will need to do some decluttering and inventorying now and then.

In this chapter, we'll go over how to do an inventory and declutter your digital life. This will need to be done regularly on your computer, phone, inbox, social media accounts, digital files, internet usage, and other devices.

Let's start with the simplest option.

How to Declutter a Computer

Your desktop computer, whether for work or at home, is a device that is easily cluttered. If it's the family computer, expect clutter to pile up quickly because everyone in the family has access to it.

Remember that the goal of a desktop declutter is to remove anything from your computer that hasn't been used in a while. This will free up some hard drive space and clear the visuals on your desktop screen.

Furthermore, there is no reason to keep files that you no longer use. It will also enable you to use your device with a purpose.

Anything that isn't adding value to your life and is simply taking up space should be eliminated.

The steps are as follows:

1. Organize your desktop.

This is usually a good place to start. It is common practice for people to download things and save them to their desktop. The reasoning behind this is that it is the first thing you see when you boot up your computer, reminding you that you downloaded your files there.

When you see your files on your desktop wallpaper, they are easier to find. That is if it was free of clutter. I started doing this after having to call Dell tech support.

To get my computer fixed, I needed to download a file or app, and the tech support guy told me to save the file on my desktop. That is exactly what I did.

Because I only had about ten icons on my screen at the time, it was relatively easy to find. It eventually became a habit, and I also forgot to delete or move almost everything I downloaded.

After more than two years, I still found that file on my desktop from the day I started decluttering my files. It was just sitting there, and I hadn't used it in a long time, so it didn't make sense to keep it.

Examine all of the icons on your desktop—all of them. If you haven't used it in the last six months, then get rid of it.

Upload it to social media or your Google Drive if it is a valuable image to you (or some other cloud storage). Keep it there, rather than on your desktop.

You can limit the number of files on your desktop to only system icons such as the Recycle Bin, Network, and Control Panel. If you have frequently used apps, folders, and programs, simply pin them to the taskbar or dock. The dock/taskbar can then be auto-hidden to keep it out of your way.

2. Replace your wallpaper

Because you're already decluttering and changing things on your active desktop, you should also change your wallpaper. Yes, it may seem insignificant, but your wallpaper can influence you positively or negatively.

If you choose a photograph that motivates you to perform better at work, that should be your wallpaper.

Now, your desktop wallpaper will not make or break your day. However, it can be a source of inspiration, which is why you should make a deliberate decision about the images you will use.

If you spend a significant portion of your day in front of your computer, changing your wallpaper now and then can be a source of motivation to begin your day. Here are a few wallpaper ideas that you might find useful to maximize the benefits of your wallpaper:

Wallpaper images that organize your desktop and turn it into a to-do list: Find a wallpaper image (or create your own) that divides your desktop screen into sections.

One section would be for icons (such as notes, tasks, videos, and so on) that you need to complete for that day. Another section would be for reminders and other information that you should read. Another section could be for things you need to do the next workday.

Choose a desktop image that allows you to organize the desktop icons on your screen logically and efficiently.

Keep in mind that you will eventually add more icons to your desktop. You might as well have a way to categorize and organize new downloads on your screen.

You should also have a section for icons that can be deleted right away. Put a download or file in that section if you don't need it and can delete it at any time during the day.

Here are some more suggestions: Workflow wallpapers, wallpapers that help you prioritize specific tasks, wallpaper organizers that will also come in handy, and to-do list wallpapers are all options.

Wallpapers for the calendar: If you're the type of person who lives and dies by their calendar, use your wallpaper as one. Editable calendar wallpapers are available for download.

These are the ones that you can change, such as whether it starts on Monday or Sunday, highlighting specific days and holidays, and adding a custom photo to the calendar that appears on your screen.

When using a calendar wallpaper, I recommend keeping your desktop as clean as possible. That means removing as many icons as possible from your desktop or simply selecting the option to hide all icons so that all you see on your desktop screen is your calendar.

Wallpapers with inspirational quotes: Having a quote-worthy statement on your desktop screen is like having a much-needed motivational speech from your coach. Sometimes a quote on your screen can inspire you and make you eager to face the day.

They can even compel you to act at times. They can sometimes serve as a pick-me-up in the middle of the week, especially when nothing seems to be going your way.

Wallpapers to help you relax: What scene gives you a sense of peace? Is it a stunning sunset at the beach, a panoramic view of the mountains, or a photograph of a local garden full of lovely flowers?

Any day can become agitating—something can happen to bring you down or make you angry. A calming and relaxing wallpaper could help you overcome any emotional highs and lows during the day. Use colored wallpapers in colors that lift your spirits. Make a desktop background out of your favorite colors.

Using color theory, keep in mind that blue color gradients can be quite relaxing. Background images with green and yellow will work well if you want to evoke happy, warm fuzzy feelings. If you're looking for colors that will give you a boost of energy in the middle of the day, look for images with red and violet as a central theme.

Images that stimulate the brain: If you need something to captivate your mind, especially when the day is getting boring, use abstract pattern desktop wallpaper. Look for fractal art, psychedelic prints, or even kaleidoscope-like patterns. They don't represent anything, but they can be pleasing and stimulating to the brain.

Scenes from nature: Nature imagery can be both motivating and inspiring to the human mind. Make your wallpaper a picture of your next weekend getaway. Your wallpaper image can also be seasonal, such as summer at the beach, rivers in the spring, beautiful falling leaves, or even snowcapped mountains. Choose nature scenes that instantly make you feel good.

Wallpaper for the minimalist: You should have expected this—yes, there are minimalist-themed wallpapers available for free download. They're extremely simple, and the aesthetics can help to drive home the goal of digital minimalism. Some minimalist wallpapers feature a single image tucked away in the screen's corner.

Sometimes it's just a single word or a motivational phrase in the center of the screen. These wallpapers contribute to the minimalist aesthetic. Furthermore, they make it easier to spot the clutter you create on your wallpaper.

Choose a wallpaper that suits you. You can even switch things up from time to time if necessary. What matters is that you keep your desktop clean. If you can maintain that for a few weeks, you'll be well on your way to digital minimalism.

3. Remove applications and programs

Apps and programs, like files, photos, videos, and other things you download, tend to clutter up your computer. You may already have some programs on your computer that you haven't used in a long time.

- Bloatware—apps that you don't need that came preinstalled with your computer when you bought it—can sometimes be found on your computer.

- Examine your list of programs. To add and remove programs on Windows operating systems, navigate to the Control Panel. But be cautious; you may uninstall something that is required for your computer system to function properly.

- If you're not a techie, there is a simpler and safer way to do it. Click on your Start screen, then scroll through the list of apps and programs that appears. Uninstall any that you no longer require or use.

- Keep your malware cleaner, antivirus software, and productivity tools up to date. You might have some games installed there, so uninstall them, especially if you're not using that computer for gaming. In any case, most people play games on their phones.

4. Make use of full-screen mode

You can work in full-screen mode with almost any app. Don't use smaller windows to split your screen. If you need to see multiple windows, I recommend using multiple screens.

Connect a second monitor to your computer to work on multiple screens. That way, you can have one document or file open on one screen and the rest of your work on another. Working in full-screen mode allows you to focus and concentrate, keeping distractions at bay.

How to Organize Your Files

After you've cleaned up your desktop and wallpaper, you can proceed to the next step: cleaning up your files. This will be more difficult because you will have more items to sort through.

Here is an observation from someone who has worked with computers for decades: as hard drives become larger, it becomes easier for people to accumulate junk. We used to work with kilobyte drives—you remember those old floppy drives?

Hard drives were then installed on computers. They were only a few megabytes in size. The most you could get back then was around 80 gigabytes, and we were already celebrating.

Then the drives grew to around 500 megabytes (while we were still celebrating—yay!). We had terabytes of hard drive space until today. People were more conscious of what they stored and saved on their computers when hard drives were smaller.

You had limited space, so you needed to make the most of it.

People no longer had to be concerned about storage space, thanks to the impending increase in hard drive space. Except you now have a lot of digital clutter. These unnecessary files slow down your computer and stifle your productivity.

Let's go over some methods for reducing the amount of digital junk on your hard drives.

1. Learn to delete the superfluous.

Keep in mind that you can complete all of these decluttering tasks at any time.

You will also be doing them regularly, so get started now. You can begin with a computer or laptop if you have one.

Keep track of how much space you've regained and how nice your wallpaper looks.

Then you can move on to your emails, phone, and other devices. It will be a difficult process for some, particularly those who have been holding onto certain files for a long time. However, keep in mind that it will be worthwhile in the long run.

2. Save files to the cloud

There will be files on your hard drive that hold sentimental value. This could include photos of your children when they were infants, photos of loved ones, documents, and files that were shared with you and have some personal significance.

So, why should you use cloud storage?

You can store your files in the cloud in a remote location that is accessible via the internet. This means that you can access your files from any device with an internet connection.

You are not limited to storing your videos, photos, and other files on a single physical hard drive, external storage device, phone, or computer. The cloud increases your productivity and efficiency.

Using this service also relieves you of the burden of maintaining your storage device. Remember that even external backup drives have a useful life of about five years.

You will need to transfer your files from one backup drive to another after five years. But what if you forget when you should do it, and your backup runs out of time? It will fail one day, and you will no longer be able to access your files.

The service providers will maintain your data and have backups of backups with the help of cloud storage, so if one of their drives fails, they will still have backups that you can use to retrieve your files.

Of course, not all cloud storage services are created equal. Some are better suited to the needs of specific people. Here are my recommendations based on your specific requirements.

Dropbox: This is, in my opinion, the best cloud storage option for light data users. It's ideal for personal use and small teams (for the free version), but they also have service plans for larger businesses. Storage options begin at 2 GB, which is quite small, but it is upgradeable. Storage plans start at $8.25 per month, making them one of the most cost-effective options.

Google Drive: This is the most cost-effective cloud storage option available today. It is free for the first 15 GB of data uploaded. You can, however, choose from larger storage space plans ranging from 100 GB to unlimited data storage. It's worth noting that the 200 GB storage space plan costs only $2.99 per month, which is quite reasonable.

Google Drive is best suited for collaborating with your work team or sharing files with family members.

Microsoft OneDrive: If you use Microsoft Windows, this may be the best cloud storage option for your device. They offer free storage for the first 5 GB of files uploaded. The paid storage plan starts at 50 GB for $1.99, making it one of the less expensive options on this list. OneDrive is also compatible with iOS and Android devices.

pCloud: If you need to store extremely large files, this is the cloud storage service for you. They offer free storage for the first 10 GB of data uploaded. For 500 GB of storage, you pay $3.99 per month. They also offer lifetime plans with a one-time fee and no recurring monthly charges.

iCloud: This could be the best storage option for iOS users because it is already built into your iPhone, iPad, or other Apple device. It's an excellent choice for private users who don't want to share their files with anyone. The first 5 GB of storage are free, and paid storage plans begin at 99 cents per month for the first 50 GB used. You can also get up to 2 TB of storage for $9.99 per month.

What you should do at this point is decide which cloud storage solution is best for you based on your specific needs. Before signing up for any cloud storage service, you should look into what their basic plans include, the upload limit, and any terms and conditions.

3. Make it easier to find your folders and files.

Which of the following folder names do you think will be easier to understand and remember:

- ✓ CB1HQ6HALH
- ✓ 2020 Work Files

You have to admit that option one above would make a great password, right? It's quite random and guessing it will be difficult. Option number two, on the other hand, will be easier to understand. The name is simple to remember and already hints at the contents of the folder.

The next step is to go through all of your folders and files and rename any that don't make sense, such as the first option in the example above. Make the names as descriptive as possible and as easy to remember as possible.

4. Minimize the number of folders

You don't need to clog your drive with specialized folders. The search capabilities of today's operating systems have been improved, making files easier to locate. You are not required to create multiple folders that contain only a few items.

For example, you could categorize all images as Photos 2020 or Photos 2019. (arranging things by year). Don't worry about the time of year because each photo you take with your device will have a timestamp, and you can arrange your photos in chronological order to make them easier to find.

In my case, I organize things by year, but you are not required to do so. It is entirely up to you how you simplify your file organization. The point is that you do not require a thousand folders on your computer. You can simply use the categories Work, Fun Stuff, and Personal Stuff to help you determine where each file should go.

5. Turn off your device and restart it.

Tell me if this is one of your habits: when you're finished with your computer, you just close it and go to bed? Do you put your computer to sleep? When was the last time you turned your phone off or disconnected it from the internet?

Here's a new habit you might like to try:

a. At the end of the day or before going to bed at night, close all open tabs, apps, and programs.

b. Move all of the files in your Downloads folder to their respective folders. If there are files there that don't belong anywhere and will never be used, simply delete them.

c. Empty the trash and recycle bins.

d. Finally, turn off your computer/phone.

This way, each time you restart your device, you're giving yourself a fresh start. If you're using your phone as an alarm clock, simply restart it.

6. Instead of purchasing digital media, rent it as much as possible.

I have a small confession to make: I still have movies and videos that I downloaded in the late 1990s. I even own the film 12 Monkeys (starring Bruce Willis).

But they're all now on a USB backup drive. I have backup drives containing over a decade's worth of videos and movies. Some of the ones I downloaded were flops, but I remember the people I watched them with back then, so it's not always about the movie.

Returning to the present, you'll notice that your computer or mobile device has a lot of digital media in the form of eBooks, videos, documents, pdf files, and so on.

Here's what I did: I stopped purchasing and downloading them. Rent it instead unless you're downloading it for your collection. Let's say you're interested in a new eBook on Amazon; don't buy it if you're not sure if it's a keeper—rent it instead.

If it doesn't work out, at least you're not filling up your Kindle library with books you've never read or have only read casually (around five or so pages). The same holds for video. Don't download videos unless you plan to watch them soon.

If you're just curious whether it's a good movie or video, rent it instead so it doesn't take up space on your device. Apply the same principle to your music and other digital media. Stream it as much as possible, and rent it if that is an option.

Cleaning Up Your Phone

You've probably already started decluttering your computer, phone, Kindle, and other devices. By now, you should have completely decluttered your laptop or computer.

We'll now move on to something a little more difficult: your phone. Our phones now play an important role in our lives. Nobody needed a smartphone, let alone an iPhone, ten to twenty years ago.

Cell phones were in the spotlight about 20 years ago, especially when Lawrence Fishbourne and Keanu Reeves starred in The Matrix movies.

Nokia was the dominant brand at the time, and flip phones were among the most technologically advanced devices available. So, even before smartphones and iPhones hit the market, people were already dependent on mobile devices—they were just not as high-tech as they are now.

Fast forward to the present; we're in a similar situation.

We still love our mobile devices, but they are more advanced and have hundreds of additional features than before.

Here are the steps to decluttering your phone:

1. Remove apps you never use.

If you've had your phone for a while, there's a good chance you have apps and games on it that you no longer use. This can include old games, alarm clock apps (in my case, I have a fart sound app that I use to prank my friends—like it's a whoopee cushion), and other apps.

2. For apps that you don't use frequently, use the web/mobile version.

Assume you don't use Facebook frequently. Maybe you just use it to check in on your friends or to pitch ideas to a group that you belong to. You don't need to install the Facebook app because you can still use your phone's browser to access Facebook.

That means one less icon on your phone's screen and one less app in its storage. Examine all of the apps on your phone and delete the ones you rarely use, opting instead for the mobile version via your browser. 3. Dock and group them

Choose three or four of your most frequently used apps. It could be your camera, YouTube, text messaging, or dialer app. After you've chosen your most-used apps, arrange them in your dock at the bottom of your phone's screen.

So, what about the rest of the apps? The rest of the apps on your phone should be grouped and stored in a folder. Put all of your social media apps in one folder, work and productivity apps in another, games and entertainment apps in another, and so on.

4. Limit the number of social media apps you use.

Believe me. You do not need to be present on every social media platform. Even if you only have a few social media apps on your device, you will live a happy life. In a later chapter of this book, we'll discuss how to wean yourself off of social media.

5. Organize your contact list

After that, go over your contact list. Go through each of the phone numbers listed there and delete the ones you never call or text. Any phone numbers that you do not intend to call again should be deleted.

If you still have music, videos, or even podcasts in your folders that you don't use or need, you should delete them as well.

6. Disable or remove any notifications

Your apps will almost certainly have notifications. Turn them off or take them out. Delete any alarms you've previously set up.

7. Establish a no-disturb time.

Setting a do not disturb time, say from 8 p.m. to 6 a.m., will allow you to sleep through the night. That means no phone calls, messages, notifications, or anything else. Putting that on your calendar will allow you to concentrate on yourself.

Clear Out Your Internet Usage

Now, here's another big step you can take: practice digital minimalism in your internet usage. When it comes to the internet, you never know how far you can fall. You may become obsessed with the latest trends. We'll go over how to do an information diet and a social media sabbatical in a later chapter of this book.

For the time being, here are a few tips to help you reduce the clutter caused by your internet usage.

1. Reduce the number of browser tabs you have open.

Internet browsers used to have only one tab. You had to open a new window if you wanted to view more than one web page. Only a few years later, browsers (beginning with Firefox) added the ability to open new tabs.

It was entertaining at first because you could open multiple tabs and such. But then, as you work, you end up with a hundred tabs open on your screen. Because opening new tabs has become so simple, you don't think about it and simply open more tabs, even if you don't need them.

What you can do is limit your use to around five tabs. The important thing here is that you select and understand what each tab contains. Don't just open tabs because you think you'll read the page later or it might have some useful information.

Close it if it's a pop-up or pop-under tab; you don't need to see or read what's on that tab.

2. Keep track of how much time you spend online.

Time Tracker is a Google Chrome extension that you can download. It is available for download from the Chrome Web Store. It assists you in identifying which websites you visit and tracking how much time you spend on various websites.

This is the first step in determining where you spend your time online and identifying time wasters. Determine which websites you spend the most time on. Then, decide which of those sites are useful and which add value to your life.

Let's say you discover you spend two hours per day on Facebook and you're old school—you still use your browser to check out your friends' posts. Assume you want to stop using Chrome for Facebook.

You can block Facebook in Chrome by installing the Block Site extension. It is a Google Chrome website blocker. Other website blockers are available, as are website blockers for different browsers.

There's LeechBlock for Firefox, StayFocusd for Chrome, Cold Turkey for Windows users, and SelfControl for Mac users to block websites.

3. Block and unfollow

Consider your newsfeed to be sacred. It isn't divine or worthy of worship, but it is something on which you spend a lot of time. If your newsfeed is clogged with things that distract you, it's time to pare down and declutter.

If someone, something, a group, or whatever it is on social media is no longer informative, entertaining, or interesting, and it is still appearing on your newsfeed, it is time to unfriend and unfollow.

Anything or anyone who does not currently add value to your life should be crossed off your list.

4. Limit yourself to one or two social media channels.

I would recommend sticking to one social media channel unless you have a specific need for another, such as Facebook for work because your boss wants you to do social media marketing there.

Only keep the social media channels that you enjoy. You have the option of deleting your account on certain social media sites, or you can simply deactivate your account. At the very least, you have the option of returning to it if necessary—say, if a client requests that you do some Instagram marketing as well.

5. Organize your bookmarks

Finally, pay close attention to your bookmarks bar. We have a habit of bookmarking web pages or websites without thinking about it. I used to have over 15 bookmark folders in my bookmarks bar, not to mention hundreds of bookmarked pages.

It's insane—I have everything from movies I want to download from Amazon to Facebook posts from friends I want to comment on later (which never happens, of course).

We bookmark pages and then promptly forget about them. We're hoping that as we go through our bookmarks, we'll remember what we were going to do with them. Unfortunately, when the time comes to search your bookmarks, you will have a difficult time finding the desired bookmarked page.

When you have a clean set of bookmarks, you are forced to be conscious of the web pages you visit. For example, if you want to open Wikipedia, you must enter the entire URL. You will be more conscious of which web pages you visit as a result.

Decluttering Your Email Inbox

According to studies, the average adult checks their email 45 times per day. If you work with emails or use them frequently in your job, you probably check your inbox more frequently than that.

Your emails aren't particularly transformative. You'll get some really important ones, but they won't come often. However, you should take control of what arrives in your inbox because going through hundreds of emails is a waste of time.

Here are some very important pointers to help you clean up your inbox.

❖ Unsubscribe from Mailing Lists

In my personal experience, I subscribed to numerous mailing lists, ranging from online courses to discount offers from various online retailers. Not kidding, my inbox once contained over 5,000 emails.

I spent a lot of time unsubscribing from mailing lists and even more time deleting emails. I had to be methodical about it. For example, I once enrolled in an email course on stock market trading. It was entertaining for a while, but then they bombarded me with promotional material, ranging from eBooks to videos. To clean up after I opted out of the service, I went through all of their emails and deleted about a hundred of them at a time. Even with that, it took a long time for me to clear out my inbox.

❖ Disable Notifications

Notifications and reminders are sent by some apps and services.

Is any of that necessary? Turn off all notifications before deleting any email reminders of this type.

❖ Create a Priority Inbox

If you use Gmail, you're missing out if you've never used a priority inbox. No, you will not lose emails when you set it up.

Using it will increase your productivity.

The priority inbox organizes all of the emails you receive into distinct categories. You have the important emails marked as read, unread, and then everything else. I used to get about 90 emails at the start of my workday.

That's a lot of emails to go through. I was able to identify the ten most important emails that required my immediate attention after activating the priority inbox. When I did that, I got more done for the day. When you enable this feature, Gmail will sort your emails by sender and subject line.

Open Gmail to enable your priority inbox. Then, select Menu (the hamburger icon), Settings, your Account, Inbox Type, and then Priority Inbox.

❖ Set aside specific times to read emails.

Consider your emails to be part of your to-do list. Never put going through your emails first. You can accomplish this by scheduling specific times to check your emails. As a general rule, you should not check your inbox every hour. Limit the number of times you check it to once or twice per day. Some people have noticed significant increases in productivity by simply checking their inbox at the start of the day and before leaving for work.

They would select one to five emails to respond to in the morning. The response should be immediate. If an inter-office email was sent and it will take you five to ten minutes to respond, it is preferable to walk over to your coworker's desk and discuss it.

I only check my email at 10 a.m. It's not the first thing that comes to mind when I walk into my office. I usually have a to-do list prepared before the day ends, and that is the first thing I go over when I arrive at work.

Then I'll pick two to three tasks that will be my top priority. Then I make plans for them for that day. I check my emails after I've allotted time for each task.

I only read the most important ones in five to ten minutes. Typically, this is only one or two emails. If I can fit the tasks and topics discussed in those emails into my schedule for that day, I add them to my to-do list (i.e., I take a minute to compose a brief and concise response to those emails).

If something important comes up that I can't fit into my schedule for that day, I put it on my to-do list for tomorrow. After that, I don't check my inbox again for the rest of the day. By doing it this way, I end up getting more done each day.

Tip:

Use a boomerang.

If you use Firefox or Google Chrome, you might want to try the free Boomerang plugin for these browsers. It's a useful tool that I discovered that has greatly aided me in managing my emails.

Boomerang lets you schedule an email to send a few days later, return an email to your inbox if the person you emailed doesn't respond after a few days, and set up other reminders to help you better manage your email activities.

Use a Pomodoro Timer as well.

We'll go over the advantages of using a Pomodoro Timer later. For the time being, keep in mind that you can use this timer (i.e., the tomato timer) to set a time limit for your email tasks.

This timer usually gives you 25 minutes to complete all of your tasks. After one Pomodoro, you should be finished with all of your emails. If you haven't finished one yet, or haven't gone through the rest of your emails, you should save them for later in the afternoon.

Unsubscribe from the vast majority of email distribution lists

Emails from lists to which you have subscribed will clog your inbox. You don't want to simply delete them when you see them in your inbox because they will continue to arrive every week.

You should open one of them, scroll down, and look at the links. Find the one that unsubscribes you from that mailing list, and then follow the prompts to complete the process.

Repeat for each email you don't want to receive. Okay, so your mother's email doesn't count. The more mailing lists you subscribe to, the longer it will take to be unlisted, but the effort will be worthwhile.

If you don't want to go through the trouble of deleting and unsubscribing from email lists, some apps will do it for you. Simply toggle the preferences and select which emails you want to delete and keep.

These are some examples of apps and tools:

- App Swizzle for iOS

- Unroll. me

- Unlisted \sUnsubscriber

Always remember to KISS.

KISS is an abbreviation that stands for "keep it short and simple." This also applies to any emails you send.

Remember to be concise when responding to emails.

This means that if you can say it in one or two sentences, it is pointless to try to convey the same message in ten sentences. Keep your answers brief. If they ask what time the meeting should be, you should give them an exact time.

There is no need to skirt the issue.

Another thing to keep in mind is that there is no need to ask your questions. If you do, you risk wasting time by replying back and forth in an email exchange. If you must communicate via email, call the other party instead. It expedites and streamlines the discussion.

Do Not Use Email as a Reminder

Some people use email as a reminder system, sending emails to themselves or asking coworkers to send them emails to remind them of upcoming meetings and other events.

If you require reminders, use your calendar. Set up reminders and other important items on your daily agenda using Google Calendar or other calendar software.

If you're tired of sacrificing productivity, wasting time, or putting up with ridiculous subject lines, the tips and tools listed here will come in handy. Your inbox should be treated with reverence. It should only include messages that are important to you.

Remember to declutter your digital life regularly. However, if you follow the best practices outlined here, everything will be much easier.

Important Takeaways

You will be conducting numerous digital inventories and decluttering tasks.

From time to time, digital clutter appears.

You must declutter various aspects of your digital life and keep track of your progress.

Chapter 4

Why and How to Perform a Digital Detox

Detoxification is the removal of toxic substances from the body. In cases of substance abuse, a person must abstain from the substance in question (such as alcohol, drugs, cigarettes, and so on). This period of abstinence allows the body to process the substances and rid itself of the toxic influence.

That is the basic medical concept behind a detox. But what about going on a digital detox? It is based on the same fundamental concept. A digital detox involves abstaining from all forms of digital technology.

Is it frightening? You're not going to use or even look at your phone for long periods? Yes, your phone, tablet, computer, TV, social media, the internet, and other forms of digital technology will be involved.

When you detox your digital life, you temporarily shift your focus away from digital technology. You can then concentrate on your day-to-day life. You will engage in face-to-face and in-person social interactions, and you will be able to do so without distractions. Consider it a digital timeout from all the tech-heavy things you do, similar to a sabbatical.

Yes, it can be frightening for some. Now, before you decide whether it is something you can do or not, think about the advantages you might gain from it. But first, you should consider what warning signs indicate that you need a digital detox.

Signs You Might Need a Digital Detox

Here is a list of the various signs that you should do a digital detox. Some of them have already been mentioned in this book.

- You can't focus on a single task for an extended period. You feel compelled to check your phone, even if only for a minute or two.

- You have a bad habit of staying up late just to play a phone game. You sometimes get up early just to play. You can't sleep unless you play on your phone before bed.

- You're afraid you'll miss out on something if you don't check social media.

- You constantly monitor the number of likes, shares, comments, and reactions to your posts.

- After reviewing your social media posts, you may become angry, frustrated, depressed, or experience other negative emotions.

- The opposite may also be true—after checking your social media posts, you may feel complete and ready to tackle whatever task you have scheduled for that day.

- You become stressed or anxious if you do not have your phone with you for a few minutes or hours. It appears that your phone (or another device) is an integral part of your identity.

FOMO (Fear of Missing Out)

FOMO stands for "fear of missing out." It is a fear that people will miss out on the best parts or events of the day. They feel disconnected from their friends, family, and colleagues if they don't participate in the latest trend, posts, or share on social media.

It's as if they must be a part of the next big trending topic or else they aren't part of the "in-crowd." In reality, they are compelled to maintain constant connectivity.

They experience this fear if they are not connected. This fear is fueled by the habit of always being connected to others via digital media. They believe their lives are less exciting without this constant connectivity (e.g., chat, posts, voice/video calls, etc.).

There may be times when you feel overcommitted to social events, whether they are face-to-face or digital meet-ups via Zoom, group chat, or other means. The overarching fear underlying it all is a sense of exclusion.

Nobody wants to be left out, do they? That is why some people feel compelled to remain connected online via digital media.

FOMO causes people to constantly check their phones, computers, or other digital devices. They don't want to miss out, so they continue to text, direct message, and post online.

A digital detox gives you the ability to limit the effects of FOMO. It does not imply that you are completely disconnected from your digital world. What you're doing is handing yourself the reins. When you check social media, you regain control of the situation, and it is not your fear that forces you to do so.

In the Digital Age, Social Comparison

In the digital age, peer pressure is real. Do you believe that peer pressure is limited to high school? It has, as it turns out, progressed to a higher plane of existence—the digital world. Doesn't that sound like Dungeons and Dragons? Consider it a kind of metaphor.

Anyway, back to the topic at hand—anyone who has spent time on social media has at some point compared their quality of life to that of their friends and family. You even compare yourself and your life to strangers such as celebrities, a famous YouTuber, or a guy who is a friend of your friend's friend who is your age and possibly in the same line of work as you.

Have you ever had the feeling that these other guys are living better and more fulfilling lives than you are? Take a look at their most recent Instagram photo carousel. Consider their wonderful vacations and the places they've visited. Take a look at their house, their pets, and their car. They're outperforming you.

Before you go any further, remember this: *"Comparison is the greatest thief of your innermost joy in life."*

A digital detox is an excellent way to remove yourself from the comparison game and focus on the life that you are currently blessed with and fortunate to have. It allows you to concentrate on what is important in your life rather than comparing yourself to others.

In short, it allows you to be content with what you have now while striving for something better.

Influence on Work-Life Balance

Constant connectivity can have a significant impact on a person's work-life balance. The amount and level of technology used are important factors in achieving that balance. Spending too much time with technology can lead to overwork, job stress, and decreased job satisfaction.

According to a study published in the journal Applied Research in Quality of Life

Constant connectivity blurs the distinction between home and work life. Because of digital technology, it is now very simple to check your emails, work files, text messages, and social media. A digital detox will allow you to draw the necessary distinctions between your professional and personal lives. It can help you reduce stress and focus on your family and personal life.

Concerns About Mental Health

According to a study published in Child Development Journal, daily heavy use of technology puts people (especially young children and adolescents) at risk for mental health issues.

According to the study, the more time you spend on digital technologies, the more likely you are to develop conduct disorder and ADHD symptoms. Another study suggests that excessive social media use increases symptoms of loneliness and depression.

According to the same study, people can reduce these symptoms by reducing their use of social media. A digital detox is an excellent way to alleviate these symptoms.

Disruption of Sleep

Do you frequently sleep with your phone next to you or in bed?

Using your phone before bedtime, according to one study, interferes with the quantity and quality of sleep. According to the same study, it has a significant impact on children. It is also suggested that heavy use of technology before sleeping is associated with a higher body mass index.

According to another study, using phones and other digital technology in bed has a significant impact on a person's mood. It also increases the likelihood of insomnia, anxiety, and sleeping for shorter periods.

Use of Digital Technology and Stress

We can already see a pattern in the studies we've cited thus far: the use of technology before bedtime, and the overuse of said technology can increase our stress levels. According to an American Psychological Association survey, 18% of adults in the United States identified technology use as a significant source of stress in their lives. This includes constantly checking emails, texting, and using social media. A study [35] involving young adults conducted by Swedish researchers confirmed the same findings.

The Phone Impact

Smartphone use reduces your ability to empathize with others. This is known as the "Phone Effect," according to experts. According to one study, the mere presence of an iPhone or smartphone can lower the quality of your conversation with others.

This occurs even if you are not using your phone while conversing with another person. The mere act of holding the phone can elicit such a reaction.

The solution is simple: leave your phone at home. Put it in your bag and go to the water cooler to speak with a coworker. It will improve the quality of your interactions and help you regain your ability to empathize with others.

How to Perform a Digital Detox

There will be many different opinions and suggestions on how to do a digital detox. Some will tell you that you must completely avoid all forms of digital media.

That means no cellphones, no emails, no social media, no internet, no TV, and so on. It would be like living as if you were stranded on a deserted island with no electricity.

Of course, living like that is nearly impossible nowadays. You can't always stay in touch with loved ones by physically visiting them. Don't get me wrong: digital technology helps us keep in touch with the people we care about and work with.

That is why I believe that digital minimalism should emphasize purposeful use of technology rather than total abstinence. It should be a deliberate, mindful, and intentional use of digital media. We must exercise self-control in how we use them.

Detaching from digital devices will improve our mental and emotional health. However, a digital detox does not imply that you will completely disconnect from technology.

Consider this: what if something goes wrong and you need to call 911? How do you do that if you get rid of your home

phone and your smartphone? A digital detox, in my
opinion, should be more about setting boundaries and
using digital devices and media in ways that benefit us.

Step 1: Be Realistic About Your Goals.

It would be ideal if you could completely avoid digital
media and technology. Even if you can only do it for one
day, you will reap some benefits from such a detox.

If you can't do it for that long, it's fine. It's also fine if you
can only partially disconnect from digital technology.
However, for many people, total separation from digital
technology is impossible. Some of us rely on it to
communicate with others, making it indispensable.

However, this does not preclude you from engaging in a
digital detox. You can still do it by limiting your use of your
phone and other devices. The key here is to disconnect and
abstain when it is convenient for your schedule.

If you need to use digital technology in your daily life—for
example, in your day job—it is acceptable to use technology
during the day. However, because you don't need it as much
after office hours, you should begin by limiting your tech
use by not checking your emails, avoiding Facebook and
other social media, and limiting your phone use to texts and
phone calls.

Step 2: Limit Your Use of Digital Technology

You can listen to music on Spotify while working, even if you're on a digital detox. As previously stated, it is critical to set limits for your digital use. I would advise you to keep your tech usage to a bare minimum—only when necessary.

Setting your devices to airplane mode is one way to limit your use of digital media. As a result, your devices are no longer connected to the internet or other wireless networks. Online messages, texts, phone calls, app notifications, social media notifications, game announcements, and other notifications will not distract you.

Disconnects should also be timed. As previously stated, you should establish when you are permitted to use digital media. When you do this, you free up your time to focus on other important issues such as your personal space, health and fitness, family, hobbies, and other personal relationships.

Here are a few ideas you might want to consider. Limit your use of digital technology at the following times:

- Before going to sleep at night

- When you first awaken in the morning

- When attending a meeting

- When you're with family and friends

- When you're catching up with friends, working on a project, or doing something you enjoy,

- When you're eating dinner

- When you're out to eat with loved ones or other important people in your life.

Step 3: Begin Slowly

You don't have to finish everything in one day. That will be difficult for some people. Begin by reducing your social media usage by 30 minutes per day for a week. According to research, doing so will improve your quality of life by reducing depression symptoms and loneliness.

So, where do you get those 30 minutes away from social media? You can begin by not using your phone before going to bed. If using your phone before going to bed is a habit, you should replace it with something else. Instead of using your phone before bed, read a book.

Do all of this for a week and try to make it a habit. It's fine if there were nights when you failed. Please forgive yourself and try again the next night. You can also reschedule your

30-minute phone-free period. If you forgot to do it before bedtime, you can do it during your morning routine—no smartphone use for 30 minutes in the morning, especially during breakfast.

Step 4: Remove Distractions

Now that you've reduced your smartphone usage, you can gradually reduce your use of digital technology. You can continue by prohibiting smartphone use at breakfast, lunch, and dinner.

You can take it a step further by removing distractions such as push notifications, unnecessary alarms, and social media alerts. Turn them all off and only keep the most important ones.

Step 5: Schedule Your Social Media Use

As I previously stated, digital technology, including social media, has its applications. Social media is one way to connect and/or reconnect with long-lost friends and family. When doing a digital detox, you want to avoid overusing social media.

Set aside specific times during the day to allow yourself to use social media. Let's say 30 minutes late in the morning and 30 minutes when you get home at the end of the day. Consider it your time to catch up with friends and family.

Step 6: Take It to the Next Level: Perform a Digital Fast

Steps 1–5 should be repeated for several weeks. After you've gotten used to the new restrictions, you can take things to the next level by committing to a one-day digital fast. It is not necessary to do it every day or every week. You can begin by selecting one day each month for a digital fast— say, the first day of each month—or perhaps the first Sunday of each month—so that you are not expecting any communication from work.

You will not touch or use any digital technology during your digital fast day. Consider it your unplugged or offline day. It's only for one day that you're completely disconnected from the internet and all forms of digital media.

Step 7: Take it a step further by observing a digital fast every other week.

After attempting a digital fast the previous month, it's time to step things up a notch. Step 6 will be repeated this time, but this time on the first and third Sundays of each month.

Step 8: Take It Up a Notch—Weekly Digital Fasts

You're going to do a digital fast once a week this time. But there will be a twist: you will get to choose which day of the week you will do it. This will necessitate a little more effort.

Step 9: Finishing Touches

You've been doing a digital detox for a while now. You already know what it's like to unplug and take some time for yourself. It's now time to hone your skills.

You may have noticed that certain activities in your digital life consume a significant amount of time. Some people spend 11 hours per week on social media, making it a bad habit.

It could be social media for some, Fortnite for others, or binge-watching TV shows on Netflix for others. Everyone's situation is unique. Determine how much time you spend on each type of digital media and technology to fine-tune your digital detox.

Choose the one on which you spend the most time. Assume it's Fortnite, and you play it for four hours every night from 11 p.m. to 3 a.m.

Sometimes you do it during the week, and sometimes you do it on weekends.

You can cut down on your Fortnite time. Assume you make it a rule not to play Fortnite on business days (Monday through Friday). You will then limit your use to weekends because you will not need to report to work anyway.

Select the app or device on which you spend too much time and limit your usage.

Step 10: Limit your time spent on social media.

People use social media all the time, even if they are hesitant to admit it. I'm not suggesting that you abandon all forms of social media. What I mean is that you should limit your use of social media by limiting the number of social media platforms you use to one or two (perhaps Facebook and Twitter). Using the strategies we've discussed here, you can also cut down on the amount of time you spend on social media.

More Tips for Digital Detox

Here are some more that may be useful to you during your digital detox. It should be noted that while some people will find it easy to give up using their digital devices and tools, others will find it difficult.

Not using a smartphone for even 24 hours can cause anxiety in some people.

Each person is unique, and sometimes people will require assistance and support to complete their tasks. As you practice digital detoxes from time to time, try any of the following suggestions:

- Inform your best friend, spouse, other friends, and family members that you are going on a digital detox. This will serve as a reminder to them to refrain from calling, texting, emailing, or sending you online messages during your digital detox hours or days.

- Keep a journal to track your progress. Someone once said that when the effort is documented, performance improves. Your success multiplies when your efforts are documented and reported back to you. One way to accomplish this is to keep a journal of your digital detox experiences and to read it at least once a week.

- Get out of the house—don't sit around doing anything. As the saying goes, the idle mind is the devil's playground. You will increase the level of temptation to use digital media when you are bored and alone. Go for a walk in the park, meet friends, have dinner with your special someone, go to the gym, walk your dog, jog, etc.

- Once you've decided to reduce the number of social media channels you use, you should go ahead and delete the apps you no longer use from your phone. For example, if you decide you no longer want to use Facebook, delete the app from your phone. This reduces the likelihood of being tempted to sign in to your account.

- Try something new. You must replace an old habit with a new one to completely break it. For example, you may have made it a rule not to use your phone after 6 p.m. That means you shouldn't be staring at your computer screen after that time. You should go do something else. Assume you heard about a new sport called Brazilian Jiu-Jitsu and thought it sounded interesting. Find a friend who wants to try BJJ with you and show up to class at 6 p.m. Doing it with someone else and setting a time limit will help you form a new replacement habit much faster.

Keep in mind that you should not rush through your digital detox. Follow the advice given here and take things slowly. Forgive yourself if you ever succumb to the temptation of spending hours on end on digital media. After that, try once more. Don't worry; it takes time for new habits to become second nature. What matters is that you never give up.

The Brain Effects of Digital Detox

In one experiment, entrepreneurs and neuroscientists were left in the Moroccan desert with no internet access.

They went on a short-term digital detox, and the results were quite interesting [37].

According to the researchers, study participants were better able to form deeper and more meaningful personal connections. When your brain is no longer overly focused on a small screen in your hand, there is a physiological benefit.

Participants reported less pain in their backs and bodies. Their digestion improved as well. Researchers attribute this to the fact that you no longer slouch and look down, resulting in better posture.

People remembered things much better because they were more present when interacting with others. Participants in the study were also sleeping better. This is because blue light from smartphones interferes with your circadian rhythm.

You can greatly improve your sleep pattern by simply doing a 24-hour digital detox. Because blue light emissions are reduced, the brain is better able to signal the release of melatonin, which causes sleep.

The World Conference on Technology, Innovation, and Entrepreneurship conducted a study on the benefits of digital detox.

Students in this study went through a brief period of digital detox.

After a brief digital detox, the male students reported feeling calmer and less stressed. This resulted in less cortisol production in the brain and other parts of the body. Female students reported that after participating in the experiment, they were better able to empathize with other students.

According to another study, a digital detox may help improve one's mood. Improving one's mood is just one of the advantages of avoiding digital technology for a short period. According to research, it may help reduce anxiety, better manage depression symptoms, and relieve eating disorders. Ways to Improve Your Life After Digital Minimalism

Here are some of the immediate advantages of a digital detox. Consider it your first experience with digital minimalism.

Allow me to list some of the advantages that such an experience can provide.

1. You determine which technologies are essential and which are unnecessary.

The first advantage of digital minimalism is that you will understand which digital media and technology are essential. You will learn how to clean up your computer and phone, and your devices will run more efficiently as a result. Aside from that, you will work more efficiently and get your life in order.

2. You Acquire Control Over Your Use of Digital Technology

You will be able to focus on those tools once you have determined which pieces of technology are critical to you and your work. You decide how and when to use digital resources, and you will make the most of them.

You don't need to have a hundred apps running on your computer and phone. You only need a few dozen or so, and you make the most of each one. You also save money because you reduce the number of monthly subscriptions you must pay.

3. You Increase Your Productivity

This relates to the previous two points raised. Because you are no longer distracted by hundreds of notifications, you become more productive. You don't need to be concerned with a slew of different work tools.

For example, if you're a graphic designer, you don't have to switch between GIMP, Photoshop, Canva, Pixlr X, and other tools. You only need to choose one or two. You become more productive, spend less time at work, and have more time for yourself.

4. You Are Not Overwhelmed

Do you recall the last time you cleaned and organized your room? Everything was calm and peaceful, and you felt better, right? That's about what you'll get if you do a digital detox and practice digital minimalism.

You no longer have any work backlogs, a large number of emails to respond to, or a stack of reports to review. There's no need to rush because everything is running smoothly.

5. You're Not Distracted Anymore

According to one expert, scrolling through endless posts, videos, pictures, and shopping items on your phone's screen is the new way we smoke cigarettes.

We've all been mindlessly scrolling through our feeds. Don't worry; I'm also guilty of doing this. You become distracted by the numerous notifications, and before you know it, you're halfway through your day with very little accomplished.

The good news is that after a digital detox and practicing digital minimalism for at least a few weeks, you will feel less distracted and have a renewed sense of purpose. You will know exactly what you want to do and when you need to complete it all.

Important Takeaways

Some indicators can help you determine whether you need a digital detox.

There are numerous negative effects of digital addiction, including those on our mental health.

When you do a digital detox, you can reduce your stress, sleep better, and focus better.

Digital minimalism has many advantages, including improved mental clarity, less distraction, and regaining control over the technology you want to use.

Chapter 5

Digital Mindfulness

The application of mindfulness practices in your digital life is known as digital mindfulness. When it comes to your use of digital technology, it entails the development of structure and routines. One of the tools you can use to eliminate interruptions and distractions is mindfulness.

What Exactly Is Mindfulness?

Mindfulness is a psychological process as well as a state of mind in which you are aware of the present moment. You achieve it by concentrating on what is currently going on around you. At the same time, you are accepting your thoughts, sensations, and feelings as they arise, calmly and consciously.

It is something you have done on occasion, whether you were aware of it or not. Mindfulness can also be used as a therapeutic practice to help people relax.

At its core, mindfulness entails accepting your memories, feelings, and thoughts without passing judgment on yourself or others as a result of them. You will allow these experiences to occur and then simply observe them. There will be no judgment about whether the thoughts, memories, and feelings are good or bad.

You also don't dwell on the past because you live in the present. You also do not focus on or imagine the future or its possibilities when you are mindful.

Mindfulness Practice's Origins

Buddhism has deep roots in mindfulness. It has been practiced by Buddhists for hundreds of years. You don't have to believe in Buddhist teachings to practice mindfulness and mindfulness meditation.

Jon Kabat's efforts and Zinn's brought mindfulness as a practice (not just meditation) to the Western world. He was an Emeritus Professor of Medicine at the University of Massachusetts Medical School. Later, he established Mindfulness in Medicine, Health Care, and Society.

He also established the Stress Reduction Clinic and pioneered the Stress Reduction and Relaxation Program. He removed the Buddhist framework from his practice, as well as any religious aspects of his clinical practice, in his work. He then renamed his stress-reduction program Mindfulness-Based Stress Reduction or MBSR.

Kabat-Zinn was able to integrate mindfulness practice into mainstream clinical practice by distancing his practice from traditional Buddhist teachings. Mindfulness is now recognized as a powerful therapeutic tool.

According to studies, meditation, specifically, mindfulness meditation, causes the brain to produce new gray matter and improves its plasticity. This is just one of many studies that show how beneficial mindfulness meditation can be.

Two Key Points on How Mindfulness Can Help You

Mindfulness, according to Kabat-Zinn, is *"...a way of paying attention in a specific way; on purpose, in the present moment, and nonjudgmentally."*

When it comes to mindfulness as a practice, two main points should be emphasized before applying it to digital minimalism.

The first point to remember is that you must learn to do things on purpose.

Mindlessness is the polar opposite of mindfulness, which means you act automatically or reactively. When something unexpected occurs, you automatically respond or use a pre-programmed response.

For example, if you have made your phone a habitual escape from boredom and sadness, the first thing you will do without thinking is reaching for your phone whenever you are bored or sad.

Some may believe that this is a quick fix for boredom, loneliness, and other negative emotions. But there is a problem with this automatic and technology-dependent response—what if the next time you pick up your phone to check your email, social media, etc., you get a negative response—negative news or posts?

Your posts are unpopular. Someone even objected to the video or image you posted. Someone even made a critical remark about it — and mentioned you. Instead of resolving your problems, it created new ones.

You can't find anything to watch on YouTube or Netflix. Nothing needs to be caught up on. There are no trends to adhere to. Instead of bringing you peace, it brings you more boredom and stress.

Mindfulness offers a solution in the form of deliberate and purposeful choice. You regain the ability to choose and human agency by doing things on purpose. You not only regain control over how to get rid of boredom, loneliness, and stress, but you also gain control over how to respond to the stimuli that cause such feelings. You address the underlying cause of the problem rather than just treating the symptoms.

According to Kabat-Zinn, the other key is to go through the experience without judgment. When you are bored, you will learn to accept the situation. But you won't be able to tell whether the experience was good or bad.

You are in the zone when you are mindful. You are in command. You are sad because of a memory that came to you as a result of a social media post. You feel it, and you are sad, but you choose not to be affected by it because you did not assess it as a negative or positive influence on you at the time.

In a state of mindfulness, all you do is go through the experience and let it flow. These emotions, memories, and experiences pass. And even after they've gone, you're still you. You are in charge, and you don't have to be depressed because you don't want to be.

You will become more aware of what is going on in your inner world—your inner dialogue—as you learn more about mindfulness and practice it in your daily life. This internal monologue is what drives you to reach for your digital technology (phone, Alexa speaker, TV, etc.).

There is a brief time and space between stimulus and response, according to best-selling author Stephen Covey. When something causes you to react, you have a brief window of opportunity to decide what to do.

Reactive people have a habitual reaction (e.g., using their phone, checking social media, listening to sad music, etc.). However, a nonreactive person (also known as a proactive person) will notice the brief period between stimulus and response. They will use that brief window to decide how to respond.

Mindfulness practice allows you to not only recognize that brief moment between stimulus and response but also to expand it. You regain your inner strength and empowerment by practicing mindfulness. You no longer need to check your emails every hour in the hopes of finding something interesting.

What people post on social media will no longer have an impact on you.

Even if no one responds to your posts, or if they do, you are not sad, angry, or resentful. You get to choose how you react to such things. Do they dislike your photograph? It's fine. You proceed.

What matters is that you did something important to you, regardless of how others reacted to it.

You are never robbed of your sense of satisfaction, contentment, or even hope. Remember that the ultimate goal of digital mindfulness practice is to allow you to slow down and fully experience life as it happens.

We have become so accustomed to a fast-paced environment that we have forgotten how to live fully. The goal of digital mindfulness is not to avoid the negative aspects of life. That is completely impossible. Things go wrong all the time, and things go right all the time.

Through mindfulness practice, you will discover that you can live in those situations while remaining calm and in control. You regain the ability to learn from these experiences and healthily deal with the negative.

Mindfulness teaches you to be mindful of all of your emotions. You learn to cope with things you used to avoid by becoming aware of and understanding them. It eventually teaches you how to deal specifically with future negativity that may enter your life.

Finally, digital mindfulness provides you with peace of mind in a constantly changing and increasingly connected world.

Mindfulness Practice in the Digital Age

Some people regard digital mindfulness as a cure for digital distraction. I'd rather think of it as one of many tools available to you. It is not the secret formula or sauce for overcoming digital technology addiction. It is not the only thing you must do to achieve digital minimalism.

Without delving too deeply into the practice of mindfulness and mindfulness meditation, here are a few things you can do right now to prepare for digital mindfulness.

We'll start with some pointers and then go over some mindfulness meditation and practices you can try.

Keep Track of Your Screen Time

Google and Apple, for example, have acknowledged that smartphone addiction is a real thing. That is why they have introduced tools that users and subscribers can use to manage their screen time.

Apple has added the Screen Time app to its iOS suite, and Google has developed Digital Well-Being Tools. These apps can help you keep track of how much time you spend staring at your phone's screen. They can also show you how many times you've unlocked your phone, how many notifications you've received, and what tools and pages you've visited, such as Chrome, Facebook, messaging, Instagram, games, and so on.

You can install these screen time apps on your phone and track how much time you spend on your device. Set a daily limit for yourself. How many times do you want to unlock your phone, how many notifications do you want per day, and how many hours do you want to spend on your phone?

You must resolve not to touch or use your phone again until the following day if you have reached any of these limits.

Turn off all non-human notifications.

Many of the notifications you receive on your computer, phone, or other devices are automatic. That is, they have been preprogrammed. There is no human being who purposefully sent it to you. These notifications were sent to you by the AI behind these programs or apps because certain conditions in their programming were met.

YouTubers, for example, usually tell you to like and subscribe to their channels, right? They also instruct you to press the bell button. You will receive automatic notifications if you click that. It's not like the owner of that channel sent you a notification that a new video had been uploaded on purpose.

Because the owner of that channel uploaded something new, the notification was sent to your device. Do you need to watch the video right now? You don't need to see it right away, so the answer is no. But you were informed, and you eventually became distracted.

The same can be said for other apps. Allowing automatic notifications from various apps will prompt you from time to time. When a timed event in a game begins, you will sometimes be notified.

What you should do is disable all notifications. You can save notifications sent by actual humans, such as emails from coworkers. However, disable all notifications from installed apps. Of course, you can keep the ones you need, such as calendar notifications and alarm clock notifications.

Set the mode to Do Not Disturb.

Examine your phone for a do not disturb or quiet mode. It will almost certainly have that option. Keep your phone in another room when you're working, teaching a class, talking to your spouse, having a meal with your family, playing music, having a one-on-one conversation with someone, sleeping, or doing anything important.

This allows you to concentrate on what you were doing. If that is not possible, set your phone to silent mode and keep it in your bag—not in your pocket or on your person. Put it in your bag and close it so you don't remember you had it in there.

Outside of the Bedroom, Charge Your Phone

When we go to bed, we all place our phones on a table nightstand so they are easily accessible. Most likely, you'll need to charge your phone before going to bed. So you leave it on your nightstand or bedside table while it charges.

A quick tip: charge your phone outside of the bedroom. You won't be tempted to grab it while lying in bed this way.

But you need your phone because it serves as your alarm, right?

Change to a standard alarm clock. It does the same thing— it wakes you up in the morning with that annoying racket. It even has one advantage in terms of digital minimalism: it lacks internet access.

The same is true for your smart speakers, virtual assistants, and other digital tools. Because those new microphones are so powerful, Alexa can hear you even if your Echo Dot 3rd Gen is outside your door.

Once a week, perform a digital detox.

We discussed doing a digital detox in the previous chapter. You should do at least one complete digital detox per week to help you practice digital mindfulness. Choose a day when you can and want to disconnect and live completely off the grid for 24 hours. You do not need to leave your house; simply disconnect everything and turn off the WiFi. If you need to go over how to do a digital detox again, please go over the discussion in Chapter 6.

Take an off-grid vacation.

Plan an off-grid vacation for your entire family. It can also be used to spend quality time with your closest friends. It could last a week or two. You should plan on going off-grid for a month if you have enough leave credits (or if your boss grants you a month-long vacation or more).

You are not required to leave the country. You can even take a vacation in the next town if there is a nature park or other place where you can stay. Enjoy nature and learn to do things without the use of technology. If you need to make a phone call, use a regular landline or a payphone.

Use this opportunity to spend quality time with the people who are most important to you.

Take a Few Mindful Moments Before Beginning a Task

Before you begin any task—taking calls, calling clients, sending emails, editing videos, starting a video meeting, writing a function in the program you were working on, and so on— You should pause for a moment to reflect. Don't just dive into the task and start hacking away. Take a moment to remind yourself of your responsibilities.

Take five deep, slow breaths. Then it's off to work. Avoid rushing so that your mind does not go into autopilot mode.

Waiting with Mindfulness

We tend to multitask in our fast-paced work environment when there is some downtime in one aspect of our work. For example, if a page we're trying to open begins to lag, we'll open another tab in our browsers to check a different page for a different task.

When this happens, we lose sight of the original task that we intended to complete. We have our attention divided, and as a result, we accomplish fewer things. We believe we are multitasking when, in fact, we are not.

Multitasking is a myth, and researchers and experts agree. What we are doing is task switching. We move quickly from one task to the next. However, this does not imply that we can perform both tasks effectively. We convince ourselves that we are multitasking. According to research, people can't focus on two tasks at the same time. This means that if you want to complete tasks quickly and efficiently, you should concentrate on only one at a time.

Interference between two or more tasks is the cause of people's inability to multitask. When you try to focus on two or more things at once, your brain begins to struggle.

That is why, instead of multitasking when you are forced to wait, take the time to do a brief mindfulness exercise. In the following section of this chapter, we will go over several mindfulness exercises. Just remember not to grab your phone whenever you hear the queue music. Take advantage of that time to meditate and practice mindfulness.

Concentrate on One Task at a Time

As previously stated, attempting to focus on a task is an inefficient way to complete it. When tempted to multitask, take a moment to consider whether you can complete one task more efficiently before moving on to the next. This will allow your mind to remain calm and clear rather than stressed out as you try to balance from one task to the next.

All things considered, unit tasking is usually the better option.

In Transition, Practice Mindful Moments

We usually jump from one task to the next as if we were on a frantic flight to complete everything. Amid the frenzy, we may fail to notice the increasing amount of tension and stress caused by the workload that has been assigned to us.

To avoid this, make conscious transitions after completing each task. For example, instead of immediately moving on to the next item on your to-do list after completing one of them, you should pause and perform a short mindfulness exercise.

Please keep in mind that this is the first of several exercises that we will go over shortly:

1. Be silent.

2. Shut your eyes.

3. Take three deep, slow breaths.

4. Notice how your lungs feel as you take each deep breath.

5. Try to remember where you are and what you just finished as you exhale.

6. Notice how you feel right now—are you cold, relieved, or still tense?

7. Let all of that emotion wash away with each deep breath.

8. Close your eyes and proceed to the next task.

It's worth noting that the preceding exercise only takes a few seconds to complete. This exercise can be done quickly before answering a client call, walking into your office, getting out of the car after arriving at an appointment, or any other time when you need a few seconds of mental clarity.

Mindfulness Exercises You Should Know

The mindfulness exercises listed below are essential for everyone, especially if you want to learn how to practice digital minimalism.

These exercises will teach your mind how to be present at the moment. They will assist you in entering a state of calm, which you will require to sort through any chaos that is currently occurring in your life.

Body Scan Workout

The body scan method is one of the first mindfulness exercises that people who want to learn mindfulness meditation will be taught. In this exercise, you will learn how to focus your attention systematically.

Don't worry, it's a simple exercise. A body scan provides you with the unique opportunity to become aware of your body and experience it as it is, without judgment. There will be no judgment on the state of your body, and you will not be required to change anything.

It will also teach you to recognize potential sources of bodily tension, discomfort, and pain. The body scan exercise is intended to help you overcome any resentments or negative feelings you may have toward your body.

You will eventually become more aware of your body's needs. You'll become more aware of its needs and sensations. It will assist you in making healthier choices regarding exercise, sleep, and eating habits.

According to one study, people who perform body scans regularly can reduce stress and improve their psychological well-being.

How to Go About It:

A full body scan can take anywhere from 20 to 45 minutes. You can, however, do shorter sessions ranging from one minute to 15 minutes. A body scan can be performed while lying down, sitting in a chair, standing up, or even walking slowly at first.

Remember that if something distracts you while performing a body scan, you should simply observe the distraction, forgive yourself for becoming distracted, and then return your focus to the part of your body that you were paying attention to.

Remember that distractions such as feelings, memories, sounds, and others are only temporary and fleeting experiences. They have no authority over you. Allow them to pass after observing them. Return to your body scan.

This is how you begin:

1. Select the most comfortable position for you (sitting, lying in bed, or standing).

2. Begin the meditation by focusing on your entire body.

3. Close your eyes if it helps you visualize your body's condition.

4. If you are seated, notice how your body weight feels on the chair. Pay attention to your body's weight on the surface you're lying on if you're lying down. If you're standing, pay attention to the sensation of your body's weight on your feet.

5. Take a few deep, slow breaths.

6. Pay attention to how deeply the air enters your body and the tension you feel in your lungs.

7. Notice how relaxed you feel as you exhale the air from your lungs.

8. Focus your attention now on your feet and legs.

9. Pay attention to how your feet feel—is there any tension?

If this is the case, try to relax your feet. Take a long, deep breath.

10. Concentrate on your legs, knees, and thighs.

Relax and release any tension in these areas of your body. Take a long, deep breath.

11. Pay attention to the muscles and tissues in your hips and buttocks. Are they tense? Take a deep breath after relaxing.

12. Now turn your attention to your stomach. Any tense muscles should be relaxed. Take a deep breath after that.

13. Repeat for your chest and back. Pay attention to how your body feels pressed against any surfaces if any.

In these areas, relax your muscles. Take a deep, slow breath.

14. Pay attention to your neck and throat. Allow them to unwind.

15. Bring your attention up to your jaw and soften that area of your body.

Pay close attention to the sensations on your face. Any tense facial muscles should be relaxed. At this time, there is no need to smile, frown, or make any other facial expressions.

Take a deep, slow breath.

16. Allow yourself to focus on the sensations that your entire body is experiencing this time. Allow your body to experience them before allowing it to relax.

17. Take several deep breaths, then open your eyes and get on with your day.

It is important to note that a shorter body scan session will only allow you to concentrate on one or two parts of your body. You get to choose which part to concentrate on.

Exercise in Mindful Breathing

This is yet another fundamental mindfulness exercise, and it is one of the first exercises taught to beginners. Mindful breathing is an excellent way to relieve stress, anxiety, and anger. After completing this exercise, you will notice that your better judgment has returned, your skills and capabilities have been reset, and you have regained your ability to pay attention and focus on things.

Mindful breathing is a foundational exercise that will be used in almost every type of mindfulness exercise. You may have noticed that you were already practicing mindful breathing in the previous exercise (i.e., body scan).

Mindful breathing separates you from your emotions and thoughts. You realize that while your feelings and experiences are a part of you, they do not define who you are.

This distance from your personal experiences allows you to tolerate negative events in your life. Mindful breathing allows your mind to focus on something specific (i.e., your breathing).

You have something to focus on, which allows you to disconnect from emotions and thoughts. You remain in the present moment and become aware of it. You are not drawn away from potentially disastrous decisions and actions.

According to one study, people who practice mindful or focused breathing become better at regulating their emotions.

How to Go About It

Depending on how much time you have, mindful breathing can take anywhere from two to fifteen minutes. This exercise should be done at least once a day, according to experts. The more you practice this exercise, the better you will become at focusing your mind and remaining mindful.

Here's how to go about it:

1. Locate a relaxing, comfortable, and quiet location where you can sit and relax. You can sit in a chair or on the floor; if you sit on the floor, please bring a cushion with you because you may end up sitting in that area for an extended period. The roof of your mouth should be occupied by your

tongue. You can rest your hands on your lap, the chair, or anywhere else you want.

2. Take a few seconds to get comfortable where you're sitting.

Be aware of the emotions you are feeling. Allow these emotions to pass.

3. Begin your mindful breathing now. Take a deep breath in and notice how the air rushes into your lungs.

4. You are not required to breathe in any way. Simply continue to breathe normally. It could be short, deep, or even rapid shallow breathing.

5. As you breathe, pay attention to how the air feels as it passes through your nose, mouth, throat, neck, and finally into your lungs.

6. Pay attention to how one breath ends and the next one begins. Pay attention to the rhythm of your breathing.

7. If anything, such as memories, feelings, sounds, or sensations, tries to divert your attention away from your breathing, give it a moment and let it pass. If you become distracted, forgive yourself and return your attention to your breathing.

8. Repeat steps 1–7 as many times as you like. It's entirely up to you. The important thing is that you can keep your attention on your breathing.

9. Continue to breathe and appreciate what you have accomplished so far. You can now get up and resume your normal life.

Walking Meditation Practice

Walking meditation is one method for practicing mindfulness even when you're on the go. You can now try walking meditations after practicing mindful breathing and body scans several times.

Walking meditations focus your attention and focus on the actual physical experience. It's something we've taken for granted. When you go on this meditative walking exercise, you will be paying attention to every movement you make with each step.

According to one study, incorporating mindful walking into your daily routine can help reduce stress, improve mental health, fight depression, and alleviate physical symptoms associated with medical conditions such as heart disease.

How to Go About It

To reap the full benefits of meditative walking, you should do it for at least ten minutes every day for a week. The more you practice it, the easier it will be to enter a mindful state in your daily life.

1. Find a nice quiet place where you can walk back and forth without being distracted. This is critical if you have never done mindful or meditative walking before.

You don't need a long lane to walk down, and you don't even need to go somewhere specific. It will be ideal to have a quiet lane on your block that is usually free of traffic. You can even do it indoors if you prefer to avoid distractions. If you do it outside, make sure there is no one around to stop you or draw your attention. Now proceed to the next step.

2. Take 10 to 15 steps forward along the path you've chosen. After completing the required number of steps, take a brief pause and then a deep breath.

3. Now turn around and walk the other way. When you get to the other end, take a deep breath and pause.

4. Now that you've walked back and forth in both directions at least once, pay attention to each step you take the next time you walk back.

5. Pay attention to how you lift your foot, how your foot lands on the ground, how you move your weight forward, how your body swings as you take each step, and how your arms move while walking.

6. Each step does not have to be completed promptly. You should walk slowly so that you can easily observe how each step is taken.

7. Instead of taking big steps, take small, shorter ones. Make it a leisurely and unhurried stroll.

8. You can clasp your hands in front of or behind you to focus solely on the movement of your feet, which makes observing your body's motions much easier.

9. Keep in mind that as you walk back and forth, your mind will eventually wander. It's perfectly natural for all of us to do so.

When your mind wanders, forgive yourself and return to observing and focusing on your body's motions as you take a relaxing stroll.

10. When you feel you've done enough walking and have a complete awareness of your body's movements, stop, take a deep breath, and then return to whatever you were doing.

For a week, practice walking meditations every day. After that, you can try it whenever you get a chance to walk.

The Raisin Method

We sometimes do things automatically, without giving them much thought. Throughout the day, we frequently enter a mindless auto mode in which we follow a habitual chain of reactions and act on preconditioned responses.

For example, when your phone rings, you instinctively reach for it and answer it, paying no attention to the wonderful technology in your hands. The cheeseburger you ordered has arrived; you instinctively dig in, bite after bite, have a conversation with your friend, and before you know it, you've finished your meal.

Have you noticed how powerful your mobile device is? Did you notice how well-made your sandwich was? This exercise will help you make mindfulness an automatic habit. You will learn to take notice of the little things and appreciate the little things in life.

This mindfulness exercise will require a prop—a box of raisins. What if you don't have raisins? Then you can use some other treat.

Choose something small, not so filling, and healthy. This exercise also teaches you to engage your different bodily senses.

It is suggested that you do this meditative exercise for five minutes every day. The steps are as follows:

1. Initial step: Gently place one raisin in the palm of your hand.

2. Take a look at the raisin you're holding. If you only want to see its features, you can hold it between two fingers.

3. Take note of how it feels in your hand. Is the surface rough, smooth, hard, or soft? Take note of how its folds and ridges appear.

Hold it up to the light to see what kind of shadow it casts. Can you see the silhouette of its internal parts if you look at it with the light shining behind it?

4. How heavy do you think it is?

5. Roll the raisin between your fingers and feel how it feels. What words can you use to describe its texture? You might want to close your eyes and visualize the surface texture.

6. Inhale the raisin scent. What does it smell like? Do you recall smelling something like that when you ate foods containing raisins?

7. Shut your eyes. Now, place the raisin between your lips but not in your mouth.

Did you notice anything? Take note of how your hand knows where your mouth is. You don't think about it; you never calculated the exact distance your hand had to travel or the precise position of your mouth about your face. You knew exactly where to place that raisin so that it would reach your lips. Furthermore, your lips know exactly how much pressure to apply to the raisin for it not to fall to the floor. You've taken your spatial awareness for granted, and now you're having to relearn it all over again.

8. Finally, pop the raisin into your mouth. But don't eat it. Take your time with it and chew slowly. Take note of the flavors you taste in your mouth. If one raisin isn't enough to let you taste the true flavor of a raisin, eat another (or two). Slowly chew and describe the taste in your mouth.

Lastly, swallow the raisin. How does it feel as it slowly enters your stomach?

This raisin method can be used to practice mindful eating.

When using this process to mindfully eat your meals, pay attention to the appearance of the food on your plate, how it feels when cut into bite-size pieces, how it smells, and the effect of the flavors in your mouth.

Method of Self-Compassion

Do you frequently replay your mistakes? Have you ever said something you later regretted saying? We all have regrets—we regret bad decisions, bad moves, bad things we did to others, poor judgment, and a variety of other things we may have caused directly or indirectly.

We dwell on the past and fail to find joy in the present, leading us to believe that our futures are bleak. Yes, it sounds mystical or even Buddhist, but these observations have roots in our current experience, even if it is modern.

This exercise will train you to concentrate on a single tangible object. You will use it to focus your attention and come to terms with your past experiences and current state of awareness.

This mindfulness exercise will allow you to take a break from punishing yourself for past flaws and mistakes. You will practice a healthier response—a compassionate response—rather than harsh self-criticism.

The following exercise will guide you through all of the essential components of self-compassion. You will learn to be mindful, kind to yourself, and have a sense of shared humanity (as defined by Kristin Neff, Ph.D., University of Texas).

Here's how to go about it:

This exercise will only take you five minutes. You can perform this exercise whenever you feel stressed or when your memories begin to haunt you, at any time of day. But, for now, you can only do it once a week.

1. Locate a quiet place where you can sit alone with your thoughts. Make yourself at ease and begin breathing slowly. Take each breath slowly and deliberately.

2. As you sit there paying attention to your breath, consider a current situation. Choose the most difficult one you are currently dealing with. 3. Try to notice if you feel any emotional or physical discomfort as you recall that problem or situation. You will usually experience symptoms such as

butterflies in your stomach, sweating, feeling cold, despair, or some other emotion.

4. Now, acknowledge that experience by saying, "I am currently suffering from this." There is no need to categorize the situation as good or bad for you. Tell yourself how you feel—"it hurts" or "I'm stressed," for example.

5. Next, remind yourself that experiencing difficulty and pain is a universal human experience. You can do this by telling yourself, "This is part of my human life." You can also say, "I am not alone; there are others who are experiencing the same problems that I am."

The important thing to remember in this step is that your suffering is not unique and that other person have or are currently experiencing the same level or amount of suffering.

6. Put your hands close to your heart, or simply give yourself a tight hug. "May I offer kindness to myself," or something along those lines, say to yourself. Similar phrases include "May I always be forgiving to myself," "May I always be patient with myself," "May I learn to accept myself for who I truly am," and "May I always be strong no matter what." You get to choose the phrase based on the dilemma or situation you are currently in.

You can do this five-minute self-kindness exercise before going to bed, when you wake up first thing in the morning, or whenever you have an extra five minutes during the day. The important thing is that you make time to be kind to yourself.

Kindness Extending Meditation

You learned how to express self-compassion for five minutes in the previous mindfulness exercise. You will complete this exercise in 15 minutes. However, there is a twist: you will also be extending kindness and compassion to others.

According to experts, people who are kind to others are more satisfied with their lives. They also have better interpersonal relationships. This type of mindfulness meditation is also known as metta meditation, and it can improve your natural ability to be kind to others regardless of your circumstances.

You can do it in the following ways:

This meditation technique will be similar to the previous mindfulness exercise. Emma Seppala, Stanford University's Science Director, created the original version of this exercise. On Dr. Seppala's website, you can learn more about its benefits and download guided meditation audio.

This exercise is divided into two parts. The first is to accept kindness and compassion and to be aware of everything you have received. The second is to spread it around so that you can bless others as well.

Experiencing Loving Kindness

1. Look for a nice, comfortable place to sit. Close your eyes and lean back on the backrest of a chair. Take a few deep breaths until you feel completely at ease. Keep your eyes closed throughout this exercise as you will go through several visualizations.

2. Consider someone close to you—someone who means a lot to you. It should be someone you know who adores you. It could be a deceased parent, the person who is currently mentoring you, your best friend, your spouse, your children, grandparents who died when you were a child, and so on.

3. Choose one of those people who care about you and imagine them sitting right beside you right now. Consider that person giving you a warm, reassuring hug, a pat on the back, or some other way of expressing their love for you.

4. Notice how warm and loving you feel as a result of the love that has been extended to you.

5. Consider another person and have them sit on the opposite side of you. Consider that person extending his or her love to you as well. There are now three people in your huddle.

6. Choose another person who loves you and imagine that person expressing love to you as well.

7. Include another person in the loving circle you are currently experiencing. Then add another, and another, until you have a group of friends and loved ones showing you compassion and love.

8. Concentrate on the loving feeling you are having at the time.

Kindness radiated

1. Now that you know what it's like to be showered with compassion and kindness by those who truly care about you, it's time for you to do the same.

2. Return to the first person you envisioned or remembered.

Consider returning that love and compassion to that person.

"Thank you for your kindness," you could say. "May you be happy and live comfortably."

3. Repeat these steps for every person in your loving huddle.

4. When you've finished reciprocating the love you've felt for everyone in your huddle, think of someone you don't know well—perhaps just an acquaintance—and send that same love to them. Consider two more acquaintances and imagine how it would feel to express your appreciation and love for them.

5. It is now time to broaden the scope of your compassion. Consider the people who may not be as fortunate as you.

Consider expressing your affection for them. Say things like, "I wish you a long, happy, and healthy life." Consider being able to assist those people in your small way. 6. Take three deep, slow breaths. When you're finished, open your eyes.

Keep track of how you feel after completing this exercise. Remember your mental state after feeling love and expressing it to others. You can always return to this experience during the day, especially when things are difficult.

How to Assist Your Family in Practicing Digital Mindfulness

When will you use these mindfulness exercises, and how will you teach them to your family? If not your family, perhaps your coworkers or office team; there will always be people with whom you can share the benefits of mindfulness in the digital age.

These mindfulness exercises can be used whenever you have free time. Instead of picking up your phone and playing a game or scrolling through social media, try a mindfulness exercise instead.

Remember that you always have a choice. Do you want the instant gratification that your digital device provides, or do you prefer the long-term peace of mind that digital mindfulness can provide? Only after you've tried the exercises described in detail above can you say that practicing mindfulness is the better option.

Here's a helpful hint: Choose mindfulness whenever you have the option of opening an email, watching a YouTube video, checking social media or using your phone. The long-term benefits of improved focus, peace of mind, reduced stress, and mental clarity are far superior.

How to Practice Digital Mindfulness at Home

It's one thing to practice mindfulness on your own, but it's quite another to get your spouse and children to join you. The first step toward teaching mindfulness to your loved ones is to practice it yourself. After you've tried it, you can tell your family about it and ask for their support.

Discuss it with them and share your experiences. Tell them about the advantages you've gotten from practicing digital mindfulness. Your spouse is the next person you should convince to join you in the practice.

You should both then set a good example for your children. You can then hold a family meeting and have your children practice it as well.

Remember to explain the benefits to them and reassure them that you are acting in their best interests as parents.

Here are some ideas for practicing digital mindfulness at home and teaching it to your children.

1. Create Mindfulness Challenges for Your Family

Children enjoy challenges and the rewards that come with them. You could have been demonstrating how to practice mindfulness. You may have even asked your children to try one of the above-mentioned exercises. They may already have an idea of what mindful living entails.

Doing mindfulness challenges as a family can be a lot of fun. For example, you could teach your children a short mindful breathing exercise and then reward them afterward.

You can also implement one of the mindful digital practices described in this chapter. You can, for example, set up screen time monitors to see if your children are spending too much time on their mobile devices.

You can agree that the child who gets the least amount of screen time during the week will get the most treats on Saturday. Of course, you must keep your promises and

prepare a surprise for them. Of course, the winner receives
the largest serving.

2. Mindfulness Huddles and Mindfulness Space

You can make a safe space in your home where people can
sit, relax, and practice mindfulness meditation. In their
homes, some people create meditation rooms or meditation
corners.

It doesn't have to take up much room. What matters is that
it is a part of the house where you can go to be alone with
your thoughts. Create it in a minimalist style. Keep the
space free of clutter and digital technology.

Because you expect the entire family to visit the area on
occasion, you should place more than one chair there. If
you don't want to set up chairs, you can lay out floor mats
and possibly some cushions where people can sit.

Once you've established your meditation corner/room, you
can plan times during the week for your entire family to
gather and practice mindfulness exercises.

These brief meetings don't have to last long. You can do it
once a week as a family and only allow 10 to 20 minutes for
the meditation session. Adjust the session length as needed.

Make it a rule that any family member is welcome to visit this designated mindfulness space. It can be your haven from the stresses, problems, and confusion of everyday life. Allow others to participate when someone comes here to meditate. You can also use the mentioned space for family meetings where you can discuss extremely important family issues.

3. Consume Mindful Meals

Remember the raisin meditation exercise we did earlier? When eating, you can apply the same mindful practices. You must skip the parts where you must put food in your hands and so on. Skip ahead to the part where you chew your food thoroughly and savor the flavors in your mouth, and revel in the sheer pleasure of good food.

However, that is not all. Because you want to keep your focus and mindfulness on the actual meal—that is, the food and the conversation at the dinner table—make it a rule that no digital technology is allowed at the table.

That means keeping the TV out of sight or turning it off while you eat. There will be no cell phones, tablets, or other electronic devices.

Everyone should concentrate on the meal and enjoy the few minutes when you can talk to the people who truly matter in your life.

4. Mindfulness and Self-Control

Let's face it: children will be children, and people will be people. Someone, somewhere, at some point, will break a mindful habit. Your child or spouse may one day spend far too much time on their smartphone.

Perhaps someone in the family will binge-watch all night.

It occurs.

Do you recall one of the phrases we keep repeating when practicing mindfulness meditation? When we make mistakes, we forgive ourselves. Extend the same level of forgiveness to others.

However, in addition to that mindfulness principle, as a parent, you should impose some form of discipline on your children to help train them not to be overly reliant on digital technology.

But how are you going to accomplish this?

Here are a few pointers:

Listen first, then inquire as to why they binged, brought their phone to the dinner table, or refused to participate in a mindful exercise with you. Don't lecture them—they don't need it. Learn to be forgiving. *"Seek first to understand before seeking to be understood,"* says Stephen Covey.

After you have fully comprehended their motivations, explain why you want them to participate in both your family's digital minimalism and mindfulness practices.

Validate their feelings and thoughts by acknowledging them. Empathize with them and try to see things from their perspective. Make it clear that you understand how they feel and think.

Redirect the conversation to demonstrate how minimalism and mindfulness can benefit them. For example, if you discover that your child stays up late at night playing phone games, here's what you can do.

After hearing what they have to say, you can explain that if they don't get enough rest, they will have trouble getting up in the morning and maybe be late for school the next day.

Show compassion and reaffirm that you care about them and that what you're doing is for their benefit.

When enforcing your house rules about minimalism and mindfulness, make it a point to reassure your children that they can confide in you. If you raised your voice, please apologize.

Make sure that whenever you give your kids pep talks, they feel comfortable opening up to you. Give them a sense of safety and reassurance that when you're being honest and open with them, they can do the same and trust you.

5. Always Understand the Rules

Your children will need to understand the boundaries you have established for everyone in the house. Setting boundaries means defining how far a child's autonomy extends, how much space in the house they are responsible for, and when and where they can use digital technology. You can discuss these rules with your children during a family meeting or in a one-on-one pep talk. The important thing is that you can establish the aforementioned house rules clearly and understandably. You can also post reminders, such as notes on the fridge or elsewhere. You can also remind your children of these rules regularly. You can hold weekly family meetings to discuss your experiences, as well as how everyone is doing with mindfulness and digital minimalism.

6. Practice Mindfulness in the Mornings

Make it a house rule that no one uses their phones or other technology for 15 minutes in the morning. Many of us have developed the habit of checking our phones as soon as we wake up.

Spending a mindful moment with your children can help them practice digital minimalism and mindfulness much better, as explained earlier in this chapter. It doesn't have to take that long—two minutes is sufficient.

If they are already holding their phones or other devices, ask them to put them down for a minute and join you in a mindfulness exercise. You only need to do the following with them [49]:

1. Shut your eyes.

2. Take slow, deep breaths in and out to clear your mind.

3. Make a note of and describe the emotions you are feeling right now. 4. Recognize and accept the emotion.

5. Take a deep breath in and out and allow these emotions to pass.

And now you can go about your morning routine mindfully. You may need to do it with your children on occasion until they can do it on their own.

Anyone who wants to practice digital minimalism will benefit greatly from practicing digital mindfulness. Minimalism allows you to disconnect from your phones, tablets, computers, and other devices, identify the underlying emotions that influence your decisions and then use technology purposefully and consciously.

Important Takeaways

Mindfulness has been practiced for hundreds of years.

The application of mindfulness principles and practices to our digital lives is what digital mindfulness is all about.

We can use mindfulness exercises at any time to regain our focus and channel it into the present moment.

We can reduce the impact and influence of digital technology in our lives by practicing digital mindfulness.

Chapter 6

More Tips and Life Hacks to Break Free from Technology Addiction

In Chapter 2 of this book, we discussed technology addiction. Many of the topics we discussed here, such as digital detoxes, decluttering, and minimalism, are beneficial in breaking the cycle of technology addiction.

In this chapter, we'll go over some life hacks that can help you break free from digital addiction.

Life Hack #1: Preventing Childhood Technology Addiction

Children are more prone to digital technology addiction, as mentioned in an earlier chapter of this book. You have the responsibility as guardians and parents to nurture and protect your children, which includes preventing digital threats.

It is easier to prevent digital technology addiction than it is to stop one that has already begun. I also recognize that it is impossible to keep technology out of our children's hands.

It is now the norm, and they will eventually use digital technology as they grow older. The smart thing to do is to train them early on to be more responsible users of digital technology.

Here are the steps you can take:

1. Observe and monitor their technology usage: You can use apps like Moment to track your children's phone usage. It can notify you when your children have spent too much time on their phones. In a previous chapter, we also discussed various screen time monitoring tools.

2. Recognize the symptoms of tech addiction: Review the symptoms and effects of tech addiction discussed in Chapter 2. If you notice two or more of the listed side effects, you should perform some direct interventions. Use the digital decluttering and mindfulness tips mentioned in this book.

3. Do not completely prohibit their use of the internet: You should never, no matter how strange it may appear, prohibit their access to the internet. Nowadays, children must learn how to use digital technology responsibly.

The internet is a modern reality, and it can be a useful tool.

What we need to teach is how to use it more responsibly.

4. Assess your child's social skills and, if necessary, provide coaching: Is your child having trouble interacting with other children? Not all children have the same social abilities. You may need to model and coach your child on how to interact with and respond to other children.

The important thing is that your child has a lot of face-to-face direct human interaction in the real world. You will also need to limit their access to the internet and digital technology. As a parent, you must identify and nurture your child's gifts and talents.

Life Hack #2: What If You Can't Live Without Technology? Tips for Using Minimalist Technology

When you need technology for work or life, how can you be a digital minimalist? I agree that it is impossible to eliminate technology in today's world. Digital minimalism does not imply abandoning technology entirely.

Here are a few pointers and ideas to consider if you require digital technology in your life:

- Don't comment on social media posts. This suggestion comes from Cal Newport's book. Don't click the like or reaction buttons, don't share the post, and don't leave comments. This could be difficult at first. The like button and other social media reaction functions are quick fixes.

- If you like what your friend posted, why not call them instead and tell them what you think? This encourages genuine, meaningful interactions and allows you to use digital technology more purposefully and mindfully.

- Combine all of your texting time. This is also applicable to chat boxes and other workplace notifications. How do you go about doing that?

- Allow your phone's airplane mode to be the default setting. Schedule 30 minutes of texting time several times throughout the day (for example, 30 minutes after lunch, breakfast, and dinner so that your meals are not disrupted).This will also teach your coworkers, staff, clients, and other associates that your time is valuable and that they cannot just barge into your day expecting an immediate response.

- Use the computer only for work-related purposes. You should only use a computer at work. There may be times when you need to use your computer for personal reasons, such as checking flights or confirming orders, but these should be limited (maybe around five to ten minutes). The goal is to limit computer use outside of the workplace. More person-to-person interactions should be prioritized in your time.

- Make use of your old alarm clock. Set an alarm before watching a YouTube video, scrolling through Facebook feeds, checking Twitter tweets, or scrolling through Instagram posts. You can spend however much time you want on social media; however, don't set your alarm for more than one hour. After you've set your alarm, go through all of your social media posts. When the alarm goes off, that's the end of it. Put your phone in your drawer and turn it off. Return to whatever you were supposed to be doing.

- But what if you use social media for business purposes? Assume you use Facebook for social media marketing and need to review your ad campaign metrics. You should bookmark Facebook for Business and use it instead of your personal Facebook account. The same feature can be found on Instagram and other social media platforms.

- Log out of your accounts and go straight to the business section of social media. You can then review your metrics, launch new ad campaigns, and fine-tune your bot settings to respond to product or service inquiries more effectively. When using social media for business, avoid using your personal Facebook account.

- Perform a digital decluttering. In chapter 3 of this book, we went over how to perform a digital declutter and inventory. We discussed how to save time on emails, how to reduce technology time, how to save time on your phone, and apps like Boomerang that will help you better manage your emails in that chapter. If you want to reduce your tech time and practice digital minimalism while still using technology, you should read that chapter.

- One day per week, completely disconnect. This is a concept that can be traced back to the Biblical Hebrews. It's known as the Sabbath. The term is

Hebrew for "rest day." It's a day when these ancient people avoid all things work-related, which is something we still do today.In his best-selling book, Stephen Covey refers to this principle as self-renewal. You take time away from the hustle of work and digital life to work on yourself.

- Set aside one day per week to disconnect from the internet and all things technological. Use that day to get a massage, learn to cook a new recipe, sleep, clean your yard, volunteer for the needy, or simply meditate and be alone to ponder on things that are important to you.

Use Art Therapy and Artistic Expression as a Life Hack #3.

Switch to actual physical art instead of using one of those coloring and art apps on your phone. Make a guitar, piano, brush, clay, or mallet your instrument, rather than any art app on your phone.

Art therapy is one option for dealing with any level of digital addiction [50]. It is a form of experiential treatment in which a person addresses their needs through creative expression.

Humans are creative beings with various modes of self-expression. Children enjoy expressing their thoughts and emotions in a variety of ways. Adults, on the other hand, can find their way of expressing themselves.

As a result, there are various types of art therapy/art expression, such as:

- Poetry

- Music/Acting

- Drawing

- Dancing

- Sculpting/Painting

Sign up for a class in one of these arts. Sign up for dance lessons if you've always wanted to learn how to dance. You can even register online. Yes, you're employing digital technology, but this time you're doing so with intention and mindfulness.

Use Mandalas for Meditation as a Life Hack #4.

Mandalas are simple to find and can be used right away.

They are those circular pattern designs that are quite captivating. Drawing and coloring mandalas can also be used as a form of meditation, allowing you to be alone with your thoughts and take some time for self-renewal.

I experimented with them and discovered that coloring them can be quite relaxing and meditative. According to research, coloring mandalas can help you practice mindfulness [51].

They're also inexpensive, and you can find a variety of patterns on Amazon or other retailers.

What you should do is as follows:

1. Purchase a mandala book online or download printable mandala patterns. If you already have some drawing skills, you can start drawing on any piece of paper.

2. Set aside an hour every day. You can schedule your mandala time twice a week or three times a week; the choice is entirely yours. If you're extremely busy, schedule ten-minute mandala sessions every day.

3. Disconnect from the internet, turn off your phone, and all digital devices (maybe just use your phone as a timer for this session).

Set your alarm for ten minutes (or whatever amount of time you've set aside for your mandala session).

4. Begin working on your mandala. Allow your thoughts to be drawn to the lines and colors in your work. Take the time to notice the patterns' symmetry. Pay as much attention to the details as possible.

5. When the alarm goes off, put your mandala somewhere safe. If you weren't able to finish the project today, you could always return to it during your next session.

6. Take several deep breaths before returning to your work or task for the day.

Learn a New Life Skill (Life Hack #5)

Choose a life skill such as cooking, swimming, biking, survival skills, self-defense, CPR, and first aid—anything that will come in handy when the time comes. This is time well spent because you are investing in yourself to become a better version of yourself.

You can enroll in a cooking class or have a friend teach you a new recipe. You are also enriching human experiences in this way. You can buy a bicycle and ask a neighbor or a close friend to teach you how to ride it if you don't know

how. By the way, you cannot learn this by simply watching
YouTube videos.

**Life Hack #6: Learn a New Skill or Talent That
Distracts You From Digital Media/Technology**

This life hack is related to the previous one in some ways.
Choose a skill or talent you've always wanted to learn. I've
always wanted to learn how to play the ukulele. So I
ordered one from Amazon and searched YouTube for
ukulele tutorials.

I discovered that the chord patterns are much easier to
remember than guitar chords because they are not as
complicated. The only issue was that I bought a soprano
that was a little too small for my hand. But I got quite good
at it.

On YouTube, there were hundreds of tutorials. The good
news is that I chose a tutorial and spent about 30 minutes
watching YouTube until I completely understood the
lesson. The best part is that I was able to cut down on my
video streaming time.

I didn't need to keep watching YouTube over and over.
After I learned that lesson, I practiced that song or chord
progression all day until I could do it with my eyes closed.

Every day, I looked forward to learning new songs. I've also discovered that digital technology can help you find something equally enjoyable.

You can do the same thing. What is something you've always wanted to try?

It could be singing, drawing, boxing, dancing, pottery, jiu-jitsu, or painting.

Choose something new to try your hand at. Use the tutorials available on the internet.

Study one lesson per day and then disconnect from the internet to concentrate on practicing what you've learned.

Continue until you have mastered that lesson. Then you can proceed to the next one.

Use Digital Technology to Reach Out and Communicate (Life Hack #7)

My team uses Zoom for meetings and presentations to clients who are located in other countries. However, that is not the only reason I use it. I usually plan virtual family gatherings. Sure, we could have done that on Facebook Messenger a long time ago, but my priority at the time was simply using social media to gain public attention.

Now, I use digital technology, specifically Zoom, to reconnect with long-lost friends and family. I don't just talk to them on Messenger; I get to see their faces and catch up with them. This is one of the positive ways to reinforce proper digital media usage. I can also use it to share files and other media that might jog my memory.

We're not just using it to fill a void in our schedule. We use it deliberately and purposefully to reach out to our fellow humans. The next time you need to use your phone, try this. Download Zoom or Lark, Google Meet, or any other online meeting app you prefer.

Plan a virtual get-together with your friends—say, the next day or an hour from now—and then go hang out with each other. Reach out to real people rather than some virtual character in a game you're playing.

Life Tip #8: Harness the Power of Grey Tones

Do you know why your phone's icons are so vibrant? That is part of the positive psychological reinforcement that causes you to tap on them. That is one of the ways they were intended to catch your eye. Keep in mind that certain colors are more likely to attract smartphone users.

Do you know what the most unappealing colors are? It's a grayscale.

According to studies, when icons are in greyscale, the positive reinforcement in the design of those icons is lost. You've taken out one of the tools that were stealing your attention.

The good news is that our devices already have greyscale color tones preinstalled. You can look for color filters in your phone's settings. Make greyscale your color scheme.

Try it out and see if you notice a decrease in your proclivity to tap icons on your phone. It's the same as turning off one of your device's pleasure switches. Because of the grey tones, using your phone is no longer as enjoyable as it once was.

Take the Time to Read a Real Physical Book (Life Hack #9)

My good friend has taken up a new hobby: reading actual books.

It all started when he saw reviews for The Wheel of Time, a new TV series (yes, he's a binge-watcher) set to premiere on Amazon. This new TV series was said to be based on a best-selling book series that spanned two decades.

How could he have missed such an important story? He wasn't a big book reader. But, after learning about the upcoming show, he wanted to be first in line. He enjoyed Game of Thrones when it first aired on television, but he never had the opportunity to read the books.

He wanted to see if he could change the experience a little this time around because it is rumored that Wheel of Time will be aired sometime in 2021. He purchased the entire 13-book set and began reading.

Some of those books were thick—really thick. The sixth book in the series had over 600 pages—man, this Robert Jordan was prolific. He went into great detail about his world, and the experience was completely immersive.

My friend is almost finished with book 6, while I am only on the first in the series. If you're reading a true page-turner, you'll be surprised that hours have passed since you first opened the book.

It's a great way to take our eyes off the screen and engage our minds. Try it.

And here's a challenge for you: read at least 30 pages per day. You can do it in one hour if you read carefully and intently.

Life Tip #10: Travel Around the World

You can overcome technology addiction by disconnecting and getting out into the real world.

Make a list of places you want to visit. Save money for weekend trips to those locations.

Going out to see the world does not limit your options to only the exotic parts of the globe. Sometimes it's as simple as getting out of the house. If you have a habit of staying indoors, spending time outside can already make a significant difference.

If you have a yard that desperately needs your attention, plan a weekend to work on it. Get your yard cleaned up and organized.

If you don't have a yard to fix and organize, you can rearrange your furniture. At the very least, you get to keep moving, which is a great way to exercise. You should, however, continue to fantasize about the places you want to visit. Plan your trips and save money for them.

QUICK TIP: Jog for 15 to 30 minutes every day, or simply walk around the block. Do it every day—every single day. If you meet someone, perhaps a neighbor you haven't seen in a while, take two minutes to introduce yourself. Enjoy the human connection.

It's a great way to meet new people while also getting some exercise. We also know that exercise helps with anxiety and depression, so you're helping yourself [52].

Lifehack #11: Use Minimalist Work Apps

Returning to digital minimalism and work, there are apps that you can use at work to help you reduce your reliance on digital technology. Several of these apps and plugins have already been mentioned in previous chapters of this book. Consider the following apps as additional resources for implementing digital minimalism at work while still utilizing technology for productivity.

Acuity

Acuity is a cloud-based appointment scheduler that integrates with a variety of services. It even integrates with PayPal and other payment platforms, so you don't have to worry about forgetting to pay your subscriptions.

Bonsai

This is a freelancer app for keeping track of your transactions. It integrates with a variety of other tools that you may already be using for work, ranging from invoice management to timekeeping.

Gaia/Easy Habit

These don't work apps, but they can be useful during breaks. During a busy day, use these apps for two to five minutes of guided meditation or mindfulness meditation. It can help bring some clarity to any difficult or difficult day.

Squarespace

This is a tool for managing email campaigns, analytics, CRM, and content marketing. It also integrates into a variety of tools, apps, and systems, eliminating the need to switch between them. Everything you need at work will be displayed on a single screen.

Offtime

This app will disable other distracting apps on your phones, such as games and social media. It will even provide analytics on your phone usage, allowing you to track how much time you spend on each of your installed apps.

Moment

This is a tracking app for phone usage that your entire family can use. Through annoying screen alerts and other notifications, it can force you to stop using your phone.

Maintain Focus

This is an Android productivity app that is useful for people who are easily distracted. This app will ask you via notifications if you are still working on a task or if you are doing something else at various times throughout the day. It serves as a reminder to get back to work.

Lifehack #12: Time Saving Office Space Hacks

According to psychologists, a cluttered environment reflects a cluttered mind. If you want to practice digital minimalism at work, you should also practice office minimalism.

Here are a few pointers:

Make use of as much white space as possible. That means there should be some space on your work desk. Maintain a white space the size of an A4 piece of paper on your dominant side.

That is, if you are right-handed, this white space should be on the right side of your keyboard. It should be on the left if you're lefthanded. This area can be used to sign papers, documents, reports, and organize documents. However, once you start doing things there, keep it clean and clutter-free.

Reduce the number of supplies on your desk. Paper clips, pens, erasers, envelopes, sticky notes, and other office supplies should not be strewn about your desk.

Do not over-personalize your workstation. Sure, having a picture of your cat or family on your work desk is nice. It motivates you to put in the effort. However, limit it to one or two personal items.

Make a file for everything. The file can be positioned on either the left or right side of your computer screen. Please limit yourself to one file. There should be a place for all papers, folders, envelopes, and work-related documents.

Set up your phone on the dominant side of your desk if you use one in your cubicle. You won't have to reach across to answer a phone call this way. You should also place it on the opposite side of the table from your keyboard so you aren't tempted to dial now and then.

The monitor should be in the center of your workstation. When you're sitting in your chair, it should be at eye level and arm's length from your body.

Chapter 7

Avoiding Relapse

It's easy to fall back into digital dependency, especially if we're just getting started on our path to digital minimalism. It won't be easy because it's very easy to open your phone and start tapping on an icon.

Here's a helpful mindfulness reminder: Even if you make mistakes and fall back into old habits, you can forgive yourself and return your attention to digital minimalism. Try not to be too hard on yourself. Remember that you are not the first person to make a mistake. Get back on track by picking yourself up.

Here are a few pointers that may assist you in avoiding a relapse.

1. Fill any available time slots

Pay attention to your idle moments as you try to develop new healthy habits that do not rely on digital technology.

Find something interesting to do to fill those downtimes.

Remember that boredom is one of the powerful influences that cause us to reach for our phones and scroll through social media, which is one of the lessons emphasized in this book.

You could spend your time cooking a nice meal for yourself and your family, reading a book, exercising, learning a new hobby, or simply trying to reconnect with friends. The goal is to stay grounded in reality and not return to your digital life.

2. Keep Track of Your Triggers

Behavioral triggers exist for habits. For example, if you are bored, your first instinct is to reach for your phone and check out the latest Instagram trend. Pay attention to these triggers and identify them for what they are.

After that, try to avoid reacting to these triggers by doing something else. The following are some of the most common triggers to be aware of:

Insecurity regarding finances

- Strained relationships

- Grief

- Depression

- Anxiety

- Fear of being overwhelmed

- Memories of trauma

- Isolation

- Loneliness

- Chronic discomfort

- Uncertainty

Mindfulness exercises can help reduce the impact of these triggers.

3. Make Contact with Someone

When you can't avoid using digital technology, use it constructively. Reaching out to someone is one way to accomplish this. Look into who you can call on Skype. Find friends on your messaging app with whom you can communicate. If you require professional assistance, ensure that you can contact your therapist online.

4. Maintain Accountability

The emphasis in tip number three is on reaching out to someone for assistance. This time, you reach out to someone to assist them. Going out of your way, even when using digital tools, requires you to be accountable for someone else.

Text messaging, phone calls, and video calls are all options. What matters is that you reach out to someone to assist them. This is an acknowledgment that being alone is difficult and that you are not alone in attempting to overcome your reliance on digital technology.

When we go out of our way to help others, our problems seem less pressing. We shift our attention away from ourselves, and in the process of helping others, we end up helping ourselves.

Important Takeaways

It is your responsibility as a parent or guardian to protect and nurture your children from negative influences, including digital technology.

When it comes to technology use, you can establish rules in your home.

Learn something new, read a book, start a new hobby, be creative, use greyscale on your phone, and keep track of your screen time.

There are strategies you can use to avoid a relapse, such as reaching out for help, being aware of your triggers, and filling up your idle time.

Conclusion

Thank you once more for your purchase of this book. I hope you enjoyed the content and that the information here was useful to you in some way. I hope you will practice digital minimalism and overcome your addiction to technology.

The following step is to implement the various tips and strategies discussed here. Being a digital minimalist takes time and practice. I recommend starting with some decluttering. That is something you will do repeatedly—trust me on that.

After that, you can practice the mindfulness exercises until they become second nature to you. Establishing and adhering to digital minimalist rules in the home and at work will take time, so be patient with yourself.

Allow yourself time to reorganize and minimize your belongings. Switching to a new minimalist approach to digital technology could be the best thing you do for yourself right now.